CW01163707

maharam

stories

first published in the united states of america
in 2015 by
skira rizzoli publications, inc.
300 park avenue south
new york, ny 10010
www.rizzoliusa.com

isbn 978-0-8478-4517-0
library of congress control number 2015932227

© 2015 skira rizzoli publications, inc.
© 2015 maharam

design irma boom

all rights reserved. no part of this publication may be reproduced, stored in a retrieval system, or transmitted in any form or by any means, electronic, mechanical, photocopying, recording, or otherwise, without prior consent of the publisher.

photo credits: 10: maharam archive; 11, 12, 13, 14: maira kalman; 18: from *flower decoration* by constance spry, 1934; 22: photograph by poul ober, courtesy de vera; 25, 26: robert ortega; 30: photograph by zeno zotti. © the solomon r. guggenheim foundation, new york, courtesy maurizio cattelan's archive; 34: © vlisco netherlands b.v.; 38: felix burrichter; 42: marian bantjes; 46: jasper morrison studio; 50: © view pictures / age footstock; 54: robert ortega; 58: henk wildschut; 62: courtesy sotheby's; 65, 66: © university of applied arts vienna, collection and archive; 70: © fondazione franco albini, milano; 74: marc camille chaimowicz; 78: © scottssweaters.com; 82: © rmn-grand palais / art resource, ny; 85, 86: robert ortega; 90: © 2015 estate of pablo picasso / artists rights society (ars), new york; 94: © sandy skoglund; 98: robert ortega; 102: liam gillick; 106: courtesy etel adnan and sfeir-semler gallery, beirut/hamburg; 110: jake evill; 112, 114:© paul p; 118: filip dujardin; 122: robert ortega; 126: © gugelot; 128, 130: paul smith; 134: courtesy michael cataldi; 138: robert ortega; 142: courtesy wright, © eames office; 146: mike abelson; 150: © the metropolitan museum of art. art resource, ny; 154: © 2013 the josef and anni albers foundation / artists rights society, new york; 158: © h.c. andersen house, odense; 162: ellen-rose smulders; 166: robert ortega; 168, 170: photograph by hisao suzuki, courtesy john pawson; 174: becca abbe; 178: courtesy studio maarten kolk and guus kusters; 182: © pierre et gilles; 186: robert ortega; 189, 190: © maira kalman; 192, 194: maharam archive, courtesy joyce friedman; 198: emily king; 202: joost grootens; 206: © 2013 doug leen and brian maebius, courtesy ranger doug's enterprises; 210: © the cecil beaton studio archive at sotheby's; 214: robert ortega; 218: photograph by poul ober, courtesy de vera; 222: natasha kroll archive, university of brighton design; 226: marian bantjes; 230: robert ortega; 234: courtesy the indianapolis museum of art; 238: robert ortega; 242: menil archives, the menil collection, houston. © a. de menil; 246: marian bantjes; 250: © scholten & baijings; 252: © lobmeyr; 254: © peter kaint/mak; 258: harmen liemburg; 262: robert ortega; 266: christoph kircherer; 270: paul p; 274: merton moss; 276, 278: irma boom; 281, 282: karel martens.

printed in italy

index

abelson	145
atlas	149
bantjes	41 225 245
beacham	213
boom	277
boyer	77
brooks	233
browne	97
burrichter	37
crawford	89
de vera	21 217
dunne and raby	117
eyck	177
gillick	101
grootens	201
heller	61
jongerius	161
kalman	13 189
king	197 221
konyha	73
liemburg	33 157 205 257
maeda	173
maharam, d	9
maharam, m	5 165 181
marbrier	265
martens	281
morrison	45
moss	29 93 273
ngo	53 241
obrist	105
p.	17 81 113 209 269
pawson	49 169
rawsthorn	25 65 69 85 109 185 261
rock	237
sagmeister	121
salisbury	153
scheltens and abbenes	57
scholten and baijings	249
sheth	193
smeets	125
smith	129
viladas	253
watson	229
willen	133
williams	137
wright	141

grommets

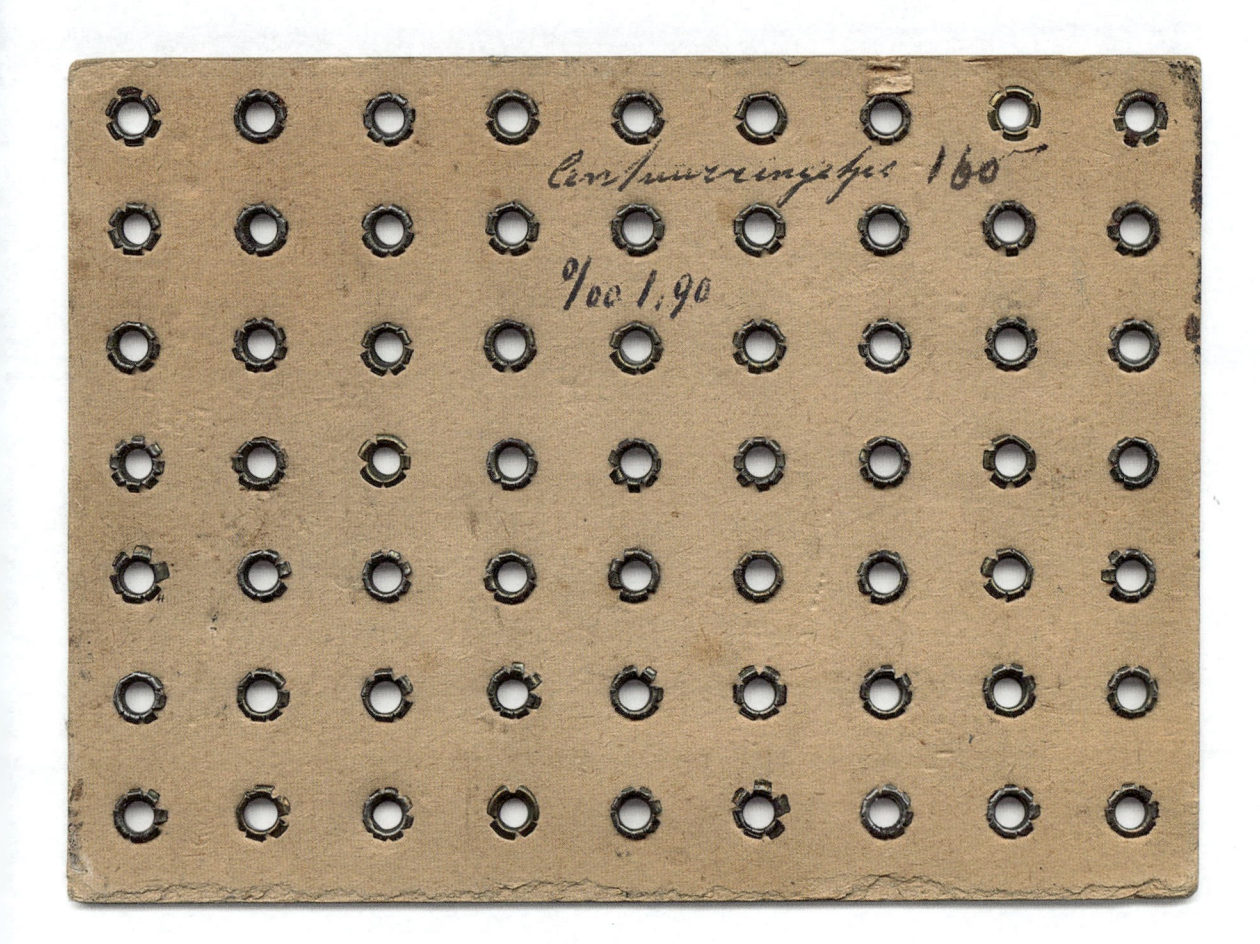

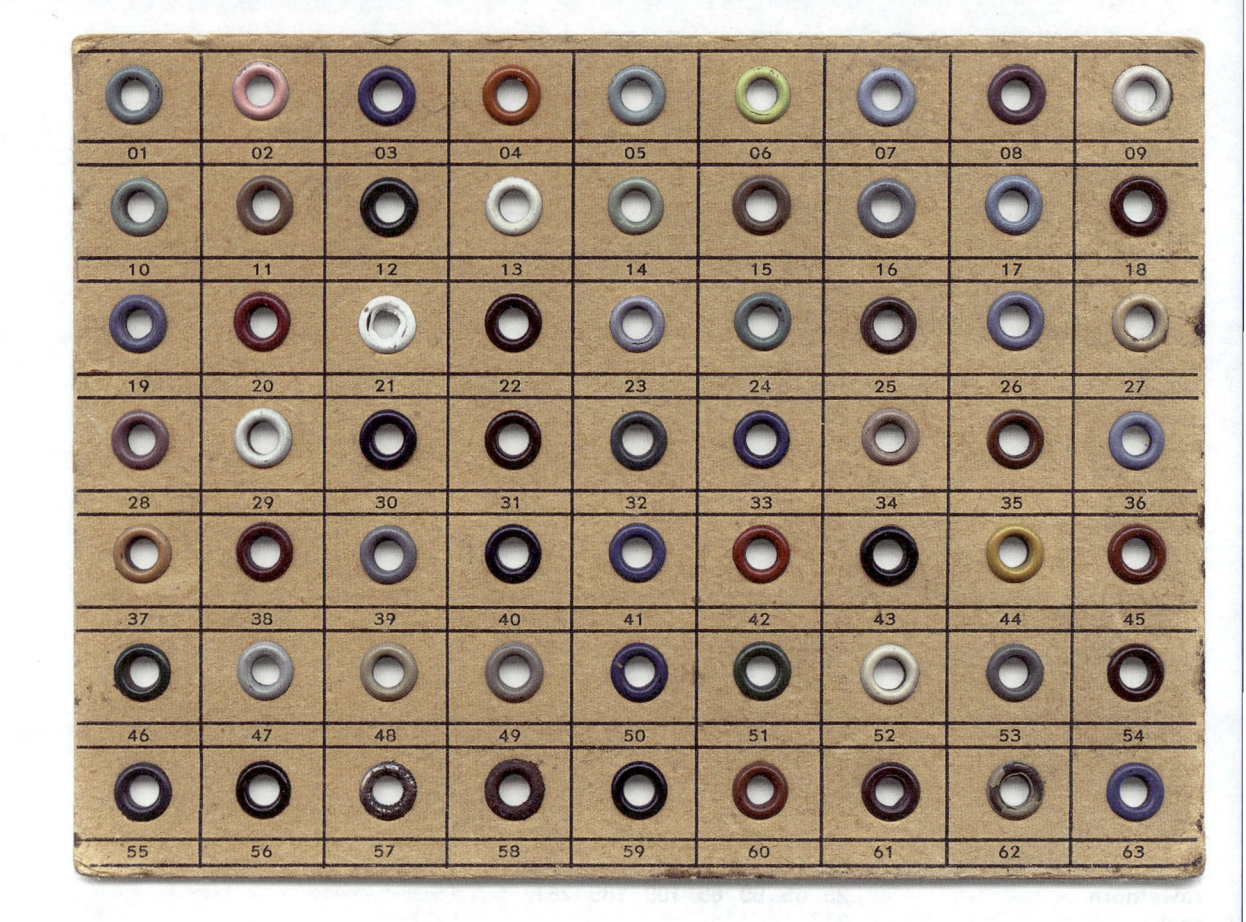

martens **karel**

print

As a designer, I respect the traditional medium of the book, but I don't let myself be restricted by it. I want to develop the medium's meaning and importance, as well as understand its limitations. Making books is about composing text, images, and information in a bound form—freezing content, in contrast to the flux of the Internet, whereby a document is created that, in turn, gives rise to reflection and encourages further investigation. In order to maintain the vitality of the book and, above all, to take the medium a step further, it is important to me that I am able to experiment freely with my designs without fear of failure. I don't allow myself to be restrained by what is technologically possible or impossible.

The materiality of the book is crucial for the experience: the choice of paper, the size of the book, the intensity of the printed colors. When one of my books is in production, I follow the printing and binding process precisely. I control the process from beginning to end. Not because of any mistrust of the printers—on the contrary, I do this more out of curiosity about what happens when the machines get started and to see what comes out after weeks, months, or sometimes years of working on a project. Even what is thrown away at the printer—what they consider wrong or not good enough—is inspiration for developing a sense of what is truly possible.

I often find myself having to defend the book as a medium and as an object, as if there is a question that books have a right to exist. I don't think they need defending: in this superficial and hasty age of the Internet, each book brings delay and depth. These are just a couple of a book's great qualities. And with the insights and innovative structures that have originated in new media, the book has received a new impetus, transforming the medium from a linear structure to something you browse through, just like a website.

The biggest threat to books seems to be the fact that people hardly read anymore, or at least much less that they did before. But I believe we are at the beginning of the renaissance of the book.

The book is dead.
Long live the book!

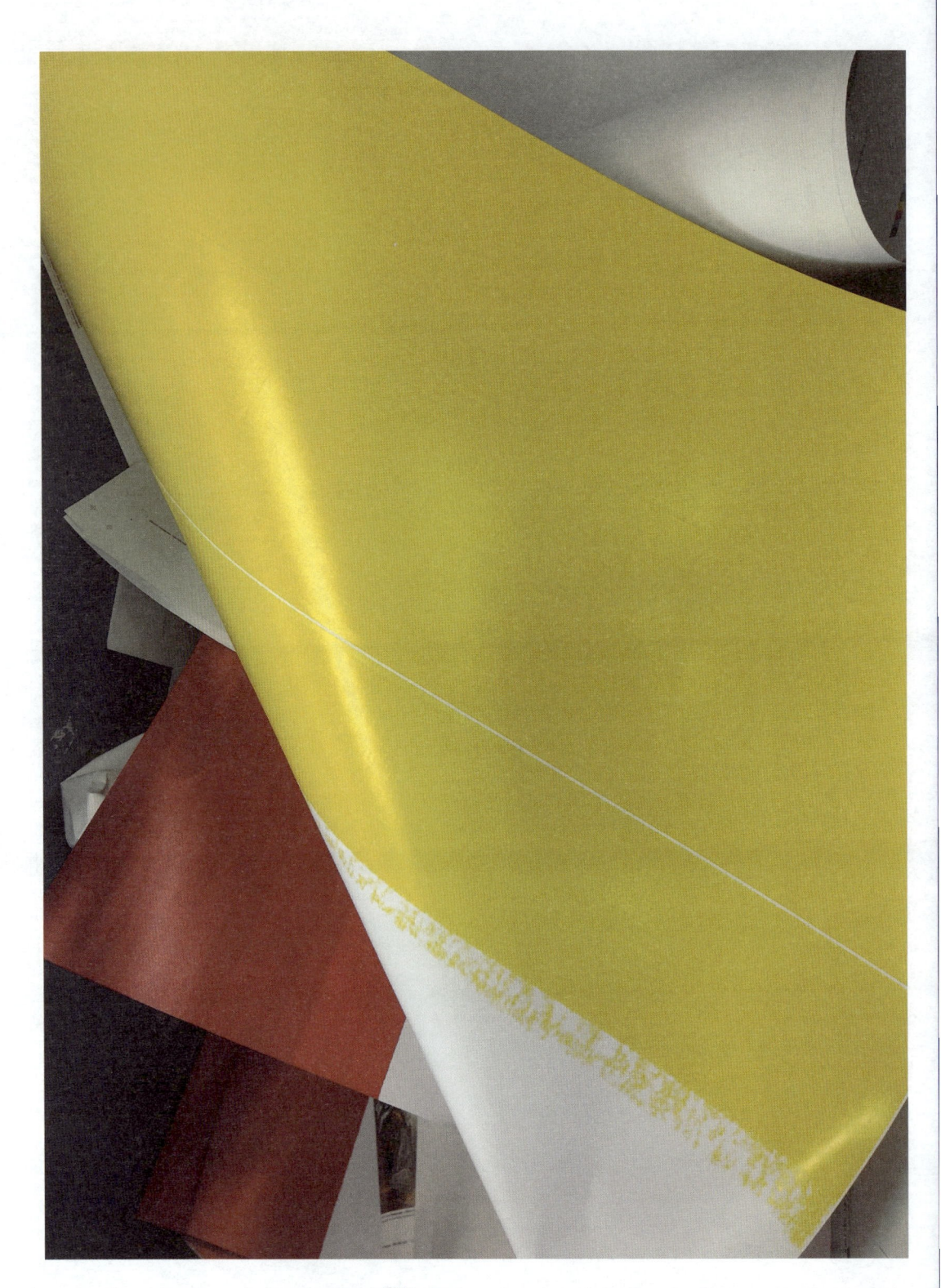

boom **irma**

hola!

The Really, Really Ugly Americans.

We were the Uber-Ugly Americans.

Touring Mexico City in our blue Cadillac, we begin to knock on doors, to "meet real Mexican families." Miraculously, we are successful in finding a family that, like ours, has a mom, dad, son, daughter. My dad, an amateur photographer, "makes an arrangement" with the Mexican dad and sets up his camera with a remote shutter release. My family and our Mexican mirror image family pose inside their home, in what is effectively a hut. Boy-girl, boy-girl, mom-dad, mom-dad. The Mexican family is staring at our clothes in the photograph; the Mexican boy and girl are nearly naked and barefoot, and my sister and I are in "authentic Mexican Junior Wear." The Mexican mom is staring at my mother's pearls. There is no judgment, no animosity apparent. Just a portrait being taken of two families, living on opposite sides of Reality. We are thrilled to be experiencing Mexico. We now have an authentic souvenir.

Five decades pass.

I am living in New York City. An old friend, running her own small agency handling marketing, PR, etc., is in a competition to win an important account—a new chain of Mexican fast-food restaurants that will be called California Burrito Co. She remembers my showing her photos years ago of the Mexico City trip, and asks if I still have any of those photos. She explains she really, really needs to win this account, and that she would like to purchase the rights to one of the images—an image of my family posing with a Mexican family in their dwelling.

She says she really, really thinks this will get her the account.

I sell her boy-girl, boy-girl, mom-dad, mom-dad for a token amount—$200. She now has exclusive rights to use that image in any way she sees fit: print advertising campaign imagery but also on T-shirts, mugs, etc. She says the image is, quote, "hilarious" in its naïve political incorrectness. It is nostalgic. It is not offensive because that picture is no longer a Reality.

About a year later I am walking down Park Avenue South and I see a fast food restaurant called California Burrito Co. I go in. I am struck dumb. I have entered Moss Family Land. There we are—everywhere—depicted on the walls in grainy black-and-white dots—blown up to movie-screen scale. There we are, and people are eating burritos and looking at us, amused.

We are not real.

We cannot be heard.

We are scenery.

California Burrito Co. closes two years later.

Evidently, something was not right.

moss

murray

Everyone likes a good "travel deal," but what would have been the "Can't Say No!" offer that would have driven you to actually purchase the Banana Boat Cruise tickets for your family holiday in Cuba, during the height of the Revolution?

Whatever that number, it was sufficiently enticing to my father (who, in all fairness, was more of an adventurer than a bargain hunter) to result in my parents, my twin sister, and me checking into the Hotel Nacional de Cuba in Havana in 1956.

It was insane.

In revolutionary Cuba, we look like decoys. CIA in "tourist costumes." My mother in her bright floral sheath dress, wearing good pearls and a hat, not to mention white gloves. My dad in his travel trench coat accessorized with his ever-present pocket protector loaded with five drippy ink pens (007? MI5?). My sister and I, looking like American Girl Deluxe Imperialist Dolls. Me: lounge wear "Cabana Set" (sports-car-printed terry-cloth jacket with golden "wheel" buttons and matching shorts). My sibling: fruit-print full skirt worn with a white off-the-shoulder "peasant blouse."

Human targets.

When we actually witness shooting for the first time, taking refuge behind a parked car, my parents understand immediately that it is not to be ruled out that WE are the target, and we literally flee to the boat.

Four years pass and we are on our way to Mexico City, driving from our home in Chicago. A very long car trip at that time, so we take the more comfortable blue Cadillac. It's summer.

Same characters as in the Cuban adventure, now circling up mountains and down mountains, vomiting the entire picturesque way into wood-grain-printed paper "burp cups" (as my mother preferred to call them).

Upon our arrival, my sister and I go "local," acquiring realistic Mexican disguises: me in a serape and HUGE straw hat, and my good-sport sister in an elaborate, heavily embroidered version of her Cuban peasant blouse and an enormous, full Mexican-print (i.e., cactus) skirt, accessorized with enormous Betty Boop gold hoop earrings.

My parents' wardrobe choices remain essentially Cuban, with one exception, lest we forget: "Mexican" handmade leather strap sandals. Just like "the locals," for the whole family!

We meant no harm. We really meant no harm. It's just that our Reality at the time put us in the Real World and all of Mexico in a diorama in the Museum of Natural History. Mexico wasn't real. The people weren't real. They couldn't hear us because they were scenery. It was Adventure Land. We were on holiday. We bought our tickets, and they didn't mind performing Mexico Land for our enjoyment.

To employ the term used to define those who, even inadvertently, exhibit ignorant, thoughtless, and ethnocentric behavior while "abroad"—a term that entered popular culture as the title of a 1958 book by William Lederer and Eugene Burdick, later made into a movie starring Marlon Brando—we were the Ugly Americans.

frederick rolfe's papal rooms

Cover all of the walls and ceilings with brown-packing paper—
yes, brown packing paper.
Stain all of the wood-work with a darker shade of brown.
The gilding of the cornices can remain as it is. No carpets.
These small greenish-blue tiles are clean; and they soothe the eye.
You may hang voluminous linen curtains on the doors and windows,
and without borders.
Furnish all those antechambers with rush chairs and oaken tables.
Remember that everything is to be plain, without ornament.
Let Us have a couch and three armchairs,
all large and low and well-cushioned, covered with undyed leather.
Get some of those large plain wooden tables which are used in kitchens.
Put writing material on one of them, there, on the right of the window.
Leave the middle room empty.
Put three small book-cases against the wall and a cupboard here.
Make a bedroom of this room.
Let the bed be narrow and long;
and let the back of the head be toward the window.
Put one of the large wooden tables here and a dozen rush-chairs.
Line the walls of this room with greenish-blue tiles,
like those on the floor.
Put several pegs on both doors.
Let a water-pipe and tap project rectangularly two feet from the wall.
Yes. Six feet from the floor, two feet from the wall; and let there be
a constant and copious supply of water—rain-water, if possible.
Get two plain oil-lamps for each room, with cooper shades:
large lamps, to give a very strong light.
Paint over both doors of the bedroom,
on the outside of each, *Intrantes excommunicantur ipso facto.*
Let Us have a plain stone altar and the stations,
and the bare necessities for mass, all of the simplest.
Let everything, walls, floor, ceiling, everything, be white—natural white,
not painted.

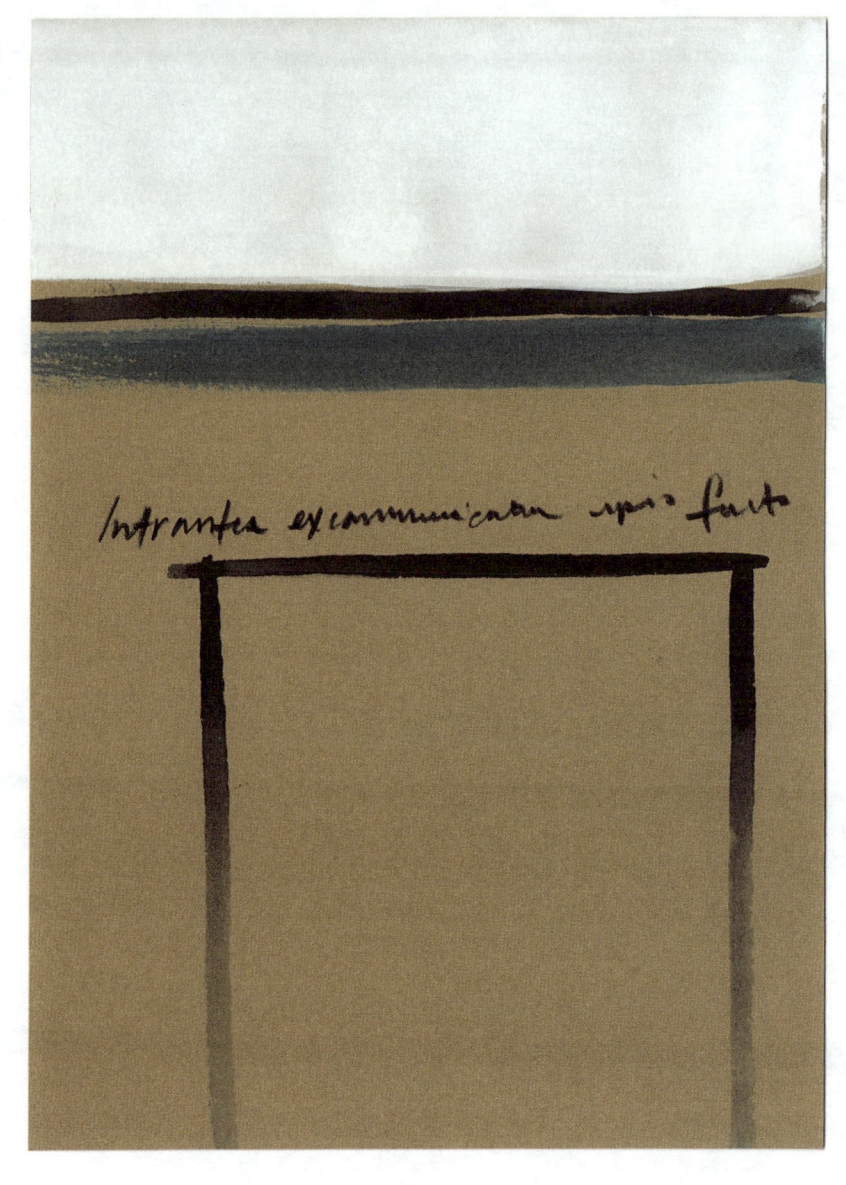

p. paul

Just as cultures are altered by the landscape in which they come to dwell, so too, in the course of a short lifetime, did Frederick Rolfe by the extreme principles of his mental atmosphere (the only air that his person could stand to breathe) find transformation, metamorphosing from a piano maker's son into the arrogant self-styled Baron Corvo.

In *Hadrian the Seventh* (1904), his novel of fantasy, Rolfe appears as the hero and ascends from London squalor to the papal throne, uniting the world momentarily through wild acts of charity, radical diplomacy, and aesthetic reform, all of which lead to his ultimate martyrdom. In reality, he routinely petitioned and was roundly refused priesthood. Denied the succor of ecclesiology, Rolfe became a penniless decadent who, if ever he found remuneration for his work, would spend it entirely on excesses and then promptly return to starvation. He either slept under the bridges of Venice or was skimmed along its canals rowed by four gondoliers, in the fashion reserved for royalty. Venice was his place of self-imposed exile. In proximity to the Vatican and among Italian youth, it was far away from the feuds and financial ruin left behind in England. It was the city for his imagination and he was a chronicler of its secret homosexual libertinism, vainly trying to pimp its dream in turgid letters sent to men back home. Rolfe was one of a type of rebel artist who, vociferously entitled and convinced of his greatness, painfully felt the failure of the world to align with his own self-image—a schism that yielded elaborately beautiful art, but also a fight to the death. Whether in poverty, or in brief fictional riches, his intransigence and contradiction of society remained the same; his actions were ruled, always, by the priority which his temperament held over his earthly circumstances.

The passage from *Hadrian the Seventh* that follows, adroit and prickling with self-assurance, describes the author's meticulous vision for an interior. Here, Hadrian commands the redecoration for the papal suite, shunning grandeur for aesthetic simplicity and nuance which, 110 years forward, we recognize, spatially and materially, as compatible with the last century's best in design theory, chiming with the clean luxury of Syrie Maugham, Jean-Michel Frank, and the utility of Bauhaus. His stream of unerring, innate taste barked out in a modern dictum is a harmonious design for living; humane, hygienic and unsuperfluous, and organized and adapted here to emphasize the pointed effect: "Now, let Us furnish these rooms."

Paul P. *Interior Color Scheme (Hadrian VII) 1*, 2014 (left)
and *Interior Color Scheme (Hadrian VII) 2*, 2014 (right).

john pawson's staircase

It already feels like another life ago when we asked our friend John Pawson to help us restore a 16th-century house in the medina of Tunis. My partner, Christoph Kicherer, and I had decided to take on a large-scale project together, and what was a better challenge than to rescue a house in a foreign country where we felt perfectly at home? I was long familiar with Tunisia; we had rented houses there for many summers, and very much by chance we found and fell in love with this one—fairly dilapidated but full of charm, located in the heart of Tunis's Medina, and surrounded by a city of two million inhabitants in a Muslim country. We'd never lived in a medina, a strange choice for a vacation home, but you can never predict a *coup de foudre*. My grandmother used to spend her winters in Marrakech in the 1960s (though in a hotel), and we had been hugely taken with the home of some Swiss friends in the medina of Lamu Town in Kenya; that was the extent of our medina experiences. Still, when you love something . . .

Just patching up the house, retaining the *World of Interiors* decrepit charm, wasn't even an option. And John was the obvious choice—Christoph was the architectural photographer John felt closest to, and it was John himself who suggested the idea from the start. For our friend, the biggest challenge was figuring out a way to get up to the terraces, given that the ground floor had twenty-foot ceilings—and my one requirement was to be able to run up and down the stairs with a tray of glasses! We decided to knock out some of the kitchen walls to make room for his sculptural stairway.

The rest is more or less history. Christoph has sadly left us. Fortunately, we still have Christoph's gorgeous photos, some lovely memories, and John's stairway to be discovered by the next generation.

marbrier   **yves**

györgy kepes's *vision + value*

Drawing on his connections in different countries, including the scientists he had encountered in London and Bass, who, as a young designer, had taken a two-hour subway ride to attend Kepes's classes in Brooklyn, he commissioned roughly a dozen essays for each of the six books. Every title addressed a different aspect of visual culture: structure, objects, movement, symbolism, repetition, and education, respectively. The contributions ranged from authoritative essays by world-renowned experts like Bronowski to the illustrator Robert Osborn's caricatures of the pain inflicted by a hangover.

As well as designing the books, each of which was nine inches by eleven inches in size with a traditional cloth binding and minimalist graphics on its jacket, Kepes wrote introductory essays for some titles and compiled eloquent image sequences. Among my favorites is his juxtaposition of traditional objects with their contemporary counterparts, such as the pairing of an ancient shell mask unearthed in Tennessee with a racing driver's helmet in *The Man-Made Object*.

Vision + Value was published nearly half a century ago, yet its contents remain compelling today, as does Kepes's central concern of nurturing new links between disciplines to address social, political, and environmental challenges. Best of all is his spirit—generous, eclectic, open-minded, and optimistic—which, exhilarating as it seems to us now, must have appeared even more so when the books were first published.

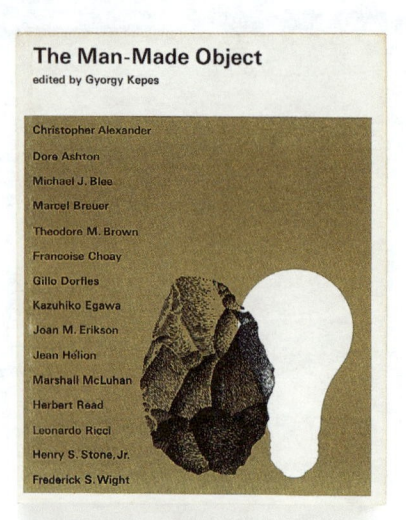

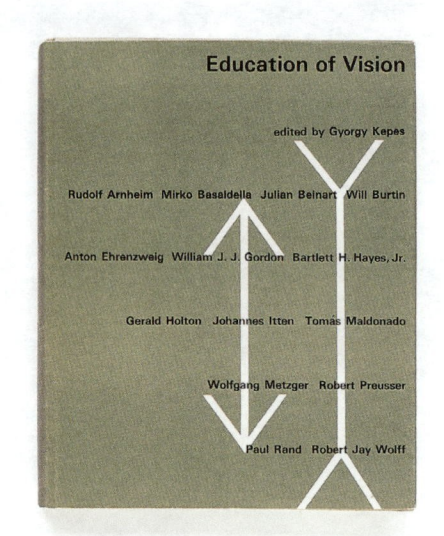

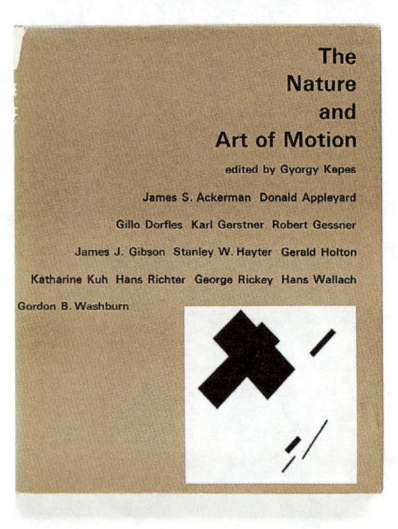

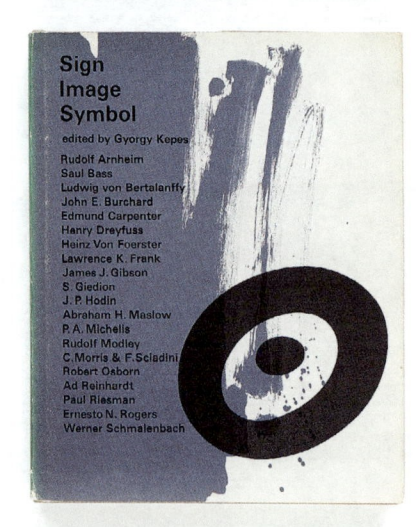

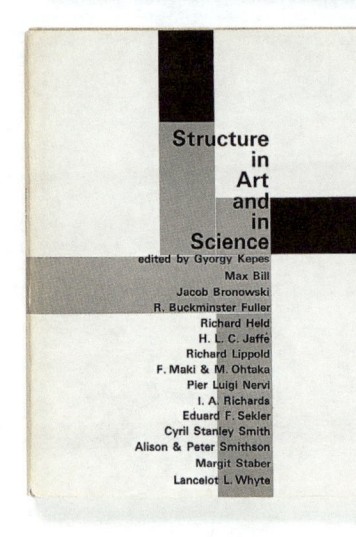

rawsthorn

alice

It would have been quite a coup for any 1960s editor to have begged, coaxed, or harried not only such eminent architects as R. Buckminster Fuller, Alison and Peter Smithson, Fumihiko Maki, and Pier Luigi Nervi into contributing to a book, but the physicist Lancelot Law Whyte and mathematician Jacob Bronowski too. And it would have been an even greater coup to have persuaded them to make their essays quite so thoughtful and provocative.

But György Kepes, who rustled up that dazzling cast of essayists for just one of the six *Vision + Value* books he compiled for the independent New York publisher George Braziller during the mid-1960s, was a remarkably persuasive man. So much so that the contributors to the rest of the series ranged from the movie title designer Saul Bass, media theorist Marshall McLuhan, and historian Siegfried Giedion to the artist Ad Reinhardt and composer John Cage.

Kepes conceived *Vision + Value* as a collective endeavour in which designers, artists, scientists, psychologists, and historians would explore ways of combining their respective skills and knowledge to visualize—and eventually realize—a better future. Dauntingly ambitious though his objectives were, Kepes was admirably equipped to realize them, thanks to the friendships he had forged in an unusually peripatetic and intellectually dynamic life.

Having mixed in Constructivist circles in Budapest as a young artist in the 1920s, Kepes fell in with the modernist movement in 1930s Berlin, where he and fellow Hungarian, the radical Bauhaüsler László Moholy-Nagy, conducted a pioneering experiments with the new genre of mechanically constructed images produced by photography and film. He then joined Moholy-Nagy and other Bauhaus émigrés in exile from Nazism, first in London, and then the United States. The two men founded an experimental design school in Chicago only for it to close after a few years. By the mid-1940s, Moholy-Nagy was terminally ill, and Kepes taught at Brooklyn College for a year then joined the Massachusetts Institute of Technology.

He and his wife, Juliet, settled into a modernist house, designed by another Hungarian Bauhaüsler, Marcel Breuer, on the northwestern coast of Cape Cod. Working alongside the scientists and technologists at M.I.T., Kepes pursued his fascination with science's relationship to art and design. He urged M.I.T. to allow him to start a new unit, the Center for Advanced Visual Studies, which would extend his research with Moholy-Nagy into the imagery produced by computers. Eventually, M.I.T. agreed and CAVS opened in 1968. *Vision + Value* was published a few years before as its unofficial manifesto.

roadside silhouettes

Throughout the western United States, the lonesome motorist will often find the endless roadside adorned with large silhouette signage, typically celebrating traditional elements of the country he is traveling through.

By far the most popular motif is the proud cowboy or rancher driving a line of cattle in front of his trotting horse. Many others celebrate the myth of settlement, with heavy oxen toiling away, pulling the settlers' wagon on the yet unpaved roads of the Wild West.

The silhouettes are made from weatherproof iron plates that were constructed using cutting torches or similar tools. Creating a graphic composition out of one sheet of material defines its own rules. If the maker is a purist, he will try to balance the positive and negative elements in an elegant way, without essential parts falling out, similar to traditional paper cuts found in Europe, China, or Mexico. But this skill is mastered by only a few patient and experienced craftsmen. More often, in order to attach smaller elements such as letters to a structural frame, the more flexible, additive strategy of welding is used.

As with any good composition, the whole is often greater than the sum of the parts. For example, the New Mexico Championship Ranch Rodeo sign —found on the road between Albuquerque and Roswell—intertwines various indigenous elements in an unusual and charming way. In it, a herd of cattle is weaving through blooming, suggesting a high-desert landscape in spring. Typical Navajo Nation triangular rug-weaving motifs are combined with elegant cursive deformed by the rugged material. Here is where rural folklore becomes Graphic Ranch Art.

liemburg

harmen

lobmeyr

In the course of my career as a design journalist, I've seen many wonderful objects. I still get a thrill from something that is intelligently designed and beautiful, too. I don't often covet these objects; I'm usually happy just admiring them. But I find it hard to remain so detached when confronted with almost anything made by Lobmeyr. The Austrian manufacturer of crystal chandeliers and other objects of desire (it is famous for its exquisitely thin "muslin" wine and water glasses) was founded in 1823, and is, crucially, still family owned and run, which allows it to treasure its heritage and nurture innovation at the same time. But rather than simply running parallel to each other, these two ideas operate in constant synergy.

Lobmeyr's offerings have long embraced both the poetically plain, like Josef Hoffmann's 1917 Drinking Set no. 238—or Patrician, as it's better known—and the beguilingly fancy, like Hans Harald Rath's exuberant Metropolitan chandelier, a glamorous 1960s starburst of brass and crystal, or Marianne Rath's sumptuous Rockcrystal bowls of 1922, which are cut with stone wheels inside and out to evoke the feeling of Renaissance rock crystal objects. The company produces masterpieces of graceful line, but isn't averse to adding a little decoration after the fact. A water tumbler from Ludwig Lobmeyr's Drinking Set no. 4, an 1856 design that is a triumph of minimalism, can also be had in a 2005 version by Sebastian Menschhorn, in which he added a seductive monogram of engraved "pearls." A few years ago, the late, lamented design store Moss had twenty of Rath's Alpha glasses —an elegantly simple 1952 design that was meant to be an accessible item for the modern table—engraved with royal monograms (including that of King Ludwig II of Bavaria) from the Lobmeyr archives.

This dialogue between the past and present precludes a slavish reverence to history for its own sake. After Adolf Loos designed his elegantly austere Drinking Set no. 248 from 1931, with its hand-cut "brilliant" base, he told Lobmeyr that he would one day like to replace the geometric pattern with images of things like butterflies or the nude human form. Decades later, the company asked the graphic designers Stefan Sagmeister and Jessica Walsh for a contemporary riff on Loos's vision, and their illustrations of the Seven Deadly Sins (and Seven Heavenly Virtues) were the basis of their 2011 Sagmeister on Loos collection. Formafantasma's delicate Alphabet glasses explore the effects of repetitive engraving patterns, managing to look both old-world and new-school. And Michael Anastassiades's Captured Light, with its light source contained in a cut-crystal sphere and hand-blown glass hemispheres, is to Lobmeyr's lighting designs what the Drinking Set no. 4 is to its glasses: an extreme economy of form underscoring the luxury of the material. Lobmeyr's continual reinvention of tradition is remarkable both for its conceptual rigor and its sensual richness, producing objects that are meticulously considered, but which still have the power to seduce.

Josef Hoffmann. Drawing of stem glasses, 1910/1913. (left)
Josef Hoffmann. Stem glasses, 1910/1913. (right)

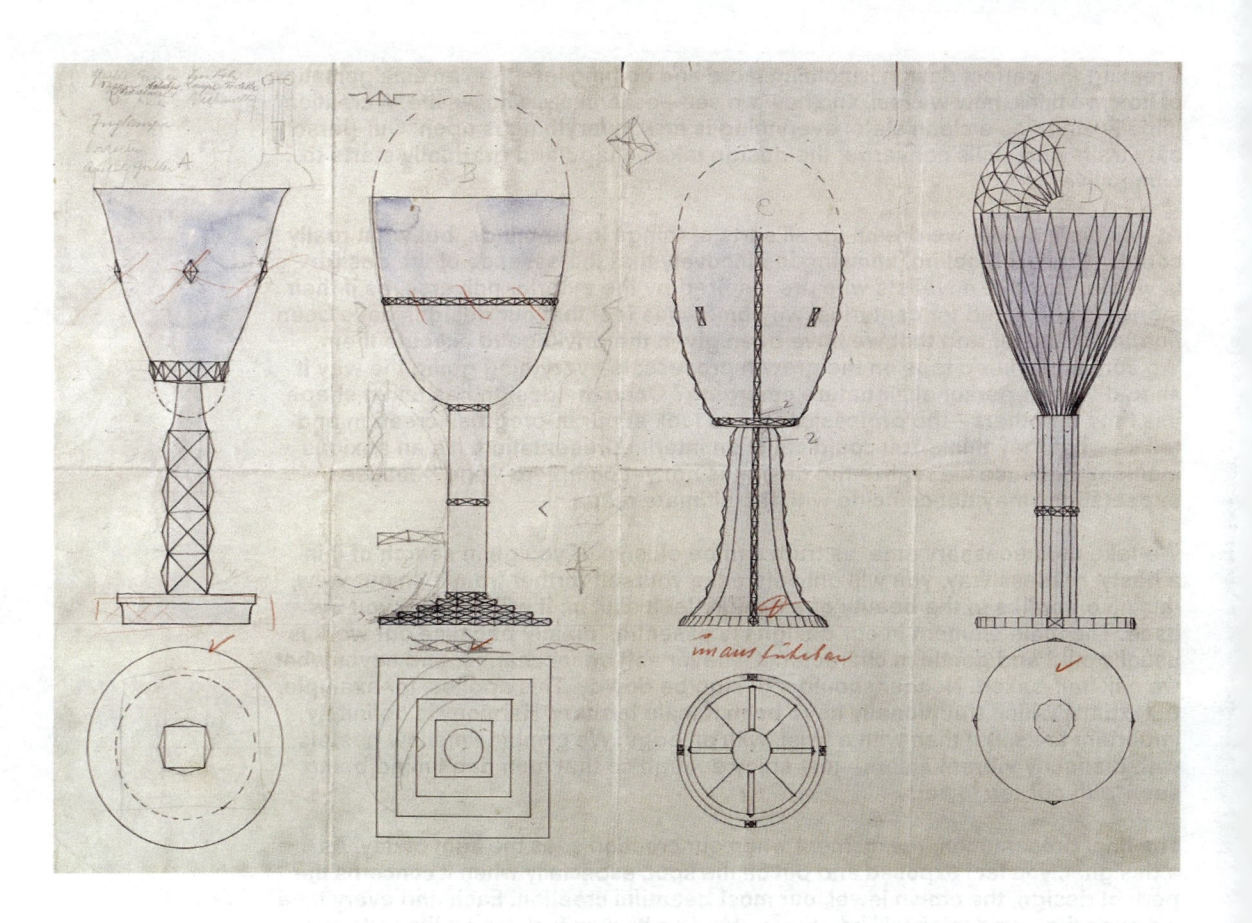

viladas **pilar**

a design with a mind of its own

Creating *the* perfect design is nothing more and nothing less than an amalgamation of how we think, how we feel, and how we see—essentially, who we are. A creation initially starts as a clean slate: everything is new, everything is open. Our personality traits and skills converge; the design takes shape and gradually starts to come alive.

At this early stage, we dream up all sorts of things in our minds, but what really counts is the gut feeling, knowing instinctively that the essence of the design is viable. Just like novelists who are inspired by the exterior universe, as if their stories had existed for centuries, we sometimes feel that our designs have been floating in the air and that we have been given the privilege to execute them. We constantly keep tabs on the growth process: Is everything going the way it should? Is our personal signature emerging? Once the design has taken shape, it is time for others—the professionals—to look at our in-progress creation and tell us what they think. You could call it an interim presentation. It's an anxious moment, because we realize the design is not yet complete—and because expectations may not coincide with the ultimate result.

We take the necessary time, as truth can be elusive. If you go in search of it in a hasty, restless way, you will only distance yourself further from it. In our view, this also applies to the beauty of a design: let it sink in; it will come to you by itself. The male element in our designs is essential, mainly because our work is usually mild and gentle in character. It's never soft or saccharine, and never what we call half-baked. Neither should a design be dowdy. This applies, for example, to textiles, which traditionally have been female territory. Harmony is definitely important to us, but then with a twist, with an edge. We combine mellow pastels with distinctly vibrant colors—just spicy enough so that men don't mind being seen with our tea towels.

The final presentation: *the* moment when our creation sees the light of day. As a designer, you feel exposed and put on the spot, especially when it concerns the perfect design, the crown jewel, our most beautiful creation. Each and every time, we hope that our design will be able to stand on its own feet, lead a life of its own, away from its makers, and that the universal beauty and strength of the design will stand the test of time.

Recently, we were deeply touched by a retrospective of our work. Each design was different, from the teacup to the bed linen, yet also very much the same. Our touch was evident in all of these products. But the elated reaction we felt on this occasion was in no way comparable to the overwhelming emotions experienced at the birth of our most perfect design. His name is Rem Martin Scholten. Now six months and sixteen days old. Will our son follow in our footsteps later on? He doesn't have to. Our perfect design has a mind of his own. But the qualities needed to become a designer were bestowed on him by nature. Open, curious, inquisitive. He explores each thread of a carpet, each hair, every leaf, flower, texture, pattern, color, and taste by touching, sampling, and looking. He does so in both a playful and serious way, with the concentration of an artist. And he remains fascinated by the wonder of it all. Each day anew. And, as with all our designs, that's what we want to continue to see—the sparkle that lights up the eyes. The joy of being alive.

scholten and baijings

stefan and carole

mother and child

The truth was she didn't love him. The baby. She was thirty-seven years old, but she felt like a relic, aged by poverty and childbearing. Twelve children, of which three had died, and now she held the thirteenth in her arms, his sticky fingers touching her face, wanting, always wanting. People admired this one for his curly locks and burnished cheeks, and she tried to humor them with a bounce for him and an indulgent smile. But she didn't feel the warmth she pretended to exhibit. At all. She had loved the first, and the second. The third, a girl, had been her favorite and the loss of her at age five had taken more from her than she could ever have imagined. By then she had had two more and was pregnant with the sixth. Something changed. Adoration turned to weary acceptance, which in turn became a hostility that she took out on her husband. Not the children—they were innocent of the grief they caused her and while she cleaned up after them and nursed them and gave more of herself than she knew she had to give, with them it was only dullness and a robotic pretense at interest that she doled out like bread. There was everyday anger, but not the deep, uncontrolled anger that welled up out of her at nights when her husband grabbed her, wanting more and still more of what little there was of her left.

It's funny what love does. She had indulged her first children with an all-encompassing absorption. Every tear and secretion from them like a part of her; her hands in their mouths, sharing food, wiping their noses, cleaning bums. But now, with this one, his wet lips and dirty hands repelled her. It was unnatural to feel this way and part of her felt ashamed and confused, but this was dampened by a lack of caring so profound and deep that even shame couldn't hide her disgust. She was his slave and would be for many years more, though thank God he was her last. For a long while she looked into his yearning eyes and considered—seriously considered—putting him down and walking away.

bantjes

marian

dominique de menil

When I was eighteen and a freshman at the Rice School of Architecture in Houston, I had to sign up for a basic drawing course. I vaguely resented this class because, like many of my dorm mates who had advanced placement credits in the sciences, I thought I should be able to bypass Drawing 101 based on my portfolio of (admittedly) self-evaluated drawings from high school. The chair of the department thought otherwise.

One night we showed up for class in our usual ratty T-shirts and cutoff shorts only to be told that we were going to an exhibition opening instead. Ten minutes later, we entered the doors of the Menil Collection, Renzo Piano's debut American project, which had just opened a few months earlier. In one corner I recognized Jasper Johns (from my prodigious high school reading of *Art in America*) talking to a slight woman with gray hair pulled into a loose bun. She was wearing a yellow silk capelike coat, which I later learned was designed by the couturier Charles James, who had also decorated her Philip Johnson–designed house. This was, of course, Dominique de Menil.

The outlines of her story are widely known: From a very well-to-do Parisian family, Dominique Schlumberger married John de Menil and the young couple migrated to Houston right after World War II, in part because of her family's oil business. The de Menils started collecting art, mostly contemporary and of their time, from René Magritte and Max Ernst in the 1940s and Joseph Cornell and Mark Rothko in the '50s to Andy Warhol in the '70s and so on. But the collection soon expanded to include tribal art and interesting, esoteric categories such as 18th-century visionary architectural drawings from the likes of Piranesi and Ledoux. When the collection got out of hand, Mrs. de Menil commissioned the up-and-coming architect Renzo Piano to design a structure to house it. It was Piano's first building in America (but his second museum, after the Centre Pompidou).

I would see Mrs. de Menil again, sometimes in the same coat but more often with her trademark dark gray shawl, at the Rice Media Center, which acted as our local repertoire cinema (and which had been originally commissioned by her to house an exhibition on early 20th-century Russian avant-garde). Based on these sightings I would venture to guess she liked Italian neorealism and early Fassbinder.

After graduation I was employed at Rice, and worked on exhibitions and publications that on occasion would bring my path to cross hers, and I would quickly learn firsthand Mrs. de Menil's unwavering beliefs in the power of art, which brings us to my favorite personal anecdote about Mrs. de Menil, from my friend Nonya, a native Houstonian: When she was eighteen, Nonya got a summer internship with Mrs. de Menil and was tasked with typing up Mrs. M's exhibition research notes onto little index cards. She was given a desk in the Philip Johnson house, and a little Olivetti typewriter. Everything was perfect for the excited young intern, except one of the typewriter keys didn't work. After a week of typed index cards missing the letter "o," Nonya nervously approached Mrs. de Menil with the problem. "Oh, I am so glad you told me—it will be fixed by the next time you are here!" she exclaimed.

The following Monday: same desk, same typewriter, same missing "o." This went on for weeks, until Nonya got up the courage to confront Mrs. M for one more time. "But of course, I promised!" she said. "Tomorrow, when you come in, this problem will have been addressed!"

The next morning: same desk, same typewriter, same missing "o." But above the offending typewriter Mrs. de Menil had hung a small, perfect Picasso.

Dominique de Menil in the galleries during the construction of the Menil, ca. 1986.

242

ngo dung

john berger: *ways of seeing*

While the digital may be destabilizing print, it is interesting to consider the reverse scenario: print *stabilizing* digital. *Ways of Seeing* was a four-part BBC television series written by critic John Berger. Shortly after it aired, in 1972, Berger and designer Richard Hollis produced a printed version of the series published by Pelican Books—a slim, five-inch-by-eight-inch paperback with only 166 pages and both black and white ink on uncoated paper—an imprint dedicated to education. The essay text starts on the cover, giving the book both a certain modesty (fewer pages) and an urgency (read it now!). The entire text is in bold sans serif, broken down into short paragraphs coupled with visual examples. Reflecting its origin as a televisual experience, the text and images work simultaneously, one leveraging the other. There are five text-and-image essays on everything from Renaissance nudes to modern advertising. But Berger also adds two entirely visual essays: a series of examples that by the power of selection and juxtaposition alone makes his thesis. In so doing he presages the development of the playlist as a predominant contemporary form and creates one of the first *pre-digital* books.

rock   **michael**

girard in needlepoint

If stripped of its furnishings, the Miller House in Columbus, Indiana, would be a relatively colorless space. It is beautifully illuminated by the skylight grid that architect Eero Saarinen and chief associate Kevin Roche created as a defining feature of the home. White Alabama marble walls faintly veined with gray, travertine floors, and white steel contribute to the sense of even light. Pale and cool, these materials might conspire to make the space austere as well. But Alexander Girard was also on the design team, bringing delight in color, texture, form, and pure whimsy sufficient to balance the intellectual rigor of high modernism with warmth and palpable humanity. Girard remained close to Irwin and Xenia Miller for many years after their house was completed in 1957, assisting with changes and refinements. In 1974, one such project was to design new cushions for the twelve dining chairs. Mrs. Miller, always keenly attuned to color, wanted something that would work with a wide variety of table settings. Family members' monograms served as the subjects for most of the group. Girard rendered them in highly stylized sans serif letters whose forms were shaped by the fine check that gave structure to both the letters and the flecks of color that enlivened the background. Cushions without monograms had an allover checked pattern. The actual needlepoint for the cushions was the work of Mrs. Miller and her bridge-playing friends —modern design meets small-town community! One can think of the cushions as a small-scale virtuoso essay in the same design dynamics that Girard used so masterfully throughout the house: vivid hues and meaningful personal expression contained within—but not diminished by—a framework of geometric precision and a background of neutral color.

brooks   **bradley**

the knob

I never actually met Lith, but I came to know her quite well.

When I first stepped into her home, some things were unforgettable: the rough-cut cedar on every wall, the clerestory windows capturing the sky, the Rothko hanging in the dining room.

Thirty years earlier, recently widowed and in her sixties, Lith had resolved to build a quiet retreat near her children. In fact, her sons and grandchildren helped with the construction of the twelve hundred square feet. But her touch was everywhere.

For a doorway, she created a set of canvases depicting the kitchen she had shared with her husband—the cupboards, the tins, her three favorite dogs (never mind that those dogs came in succession in the real world). At the entry garden, a collection of thirty varieties of fern; inside, the closet floors all hand painted. And over the rear deck, a hawthorn pruned into an impossible shape, perhaps inspired by the Japanese garden down the path and across the ravine.

But it was the knobs that sold me.

Lith's husband, George, had run a metal foundry. He was gone, but she had brought his memory with her to Raleigh Street with the hardware: hundreds of brass fixtures, knobs, and fittings. Brass towel bars, robe hooks, door pulls. Even the toilet-paper holder. And so it was unquestioned, as I moved through the restoration, that the knobs would remain. Unlacquered, those with the heaviest use had taken on a shine; the less frequented cupboards stood quietly matte —nearly green.

When I left that house, seven years on, I thought about packing up one or two of the unused knobs as keepsakes. In the end it didn't feel right to remove them. But I didn't forget them.

Years later, I found myself in another state, again restoring a twelve-hundred-square-foot home. I found myself calling Charlie, my old neighbor on Raleigh Street. Did he have a contact for the new owners of Lith's house? Did he think they might consider loaning me a brass knob so I could make a master, and cast copies for my new home? But there was no need for that effort. An exhaustive renovation by the new owners had gutted the interior. Nothing original was left.

However, for some reason, Charlie himself had rescued that hardware. A decade on, it was still sitting in boxes in his workshop—he would send it right out to me. Why he had saved it? He couldn't say.

But to me the answer was clear. Lith had wanted me to have them.

watson   **ben**

another day in the city

She was still high. She'd got some sleep—she wasn't sure how much, because she had no idea when she'd passed out—but she woke up at seven o'clock as usual, and stumbled around to find her clothes. What a mess—not the place, though that too, but her head and, really, her life. She didn't even know how she got away with it, showing up to work in the same clothes she wore the day before, smelling like smoke and booze and who knows what, though she tried to mask it with hairspray, perfume, and mints. Always lots of mints. But she'd come to realized that although she imagined every eye upon her, noticing her cracks, the glaze on her eyes, her stumbling ineptitude, the fact was that most people really *didn't* notice. People were actually completely self-absorbed with their own lives and worries and problems. As was she, come to think of it. John, in the cubicle next to hers, what did she know of him, really? Did he wear the same clothes, day after day? She actually had no idea. What was Margie wearing yesterday? What was Margie's performance? Was she on the ball? They could all be on drugs or drunk for all she knew, and it was almost with horror that she realized that she would have to fall far to catch their attention. She wondered what it would take and thought that *so long as she showed up on time* she could get away with this and a lot more. Wasn't that the ridiculous thing: it was only her prompt attendance that was an indicator of normalcy. She could be stoned, drunk, a perfect zombie and keep her job, while John there—diligently working, counting, noting—could lose his job just for being late a few days. It made her laugh. But she'd go home tonight, she promised herself. Get a decent night's sleep for a change. A couple of glasses of wine and some TV, wash her hair and put some curlers in. A proper night in. It would do her good.

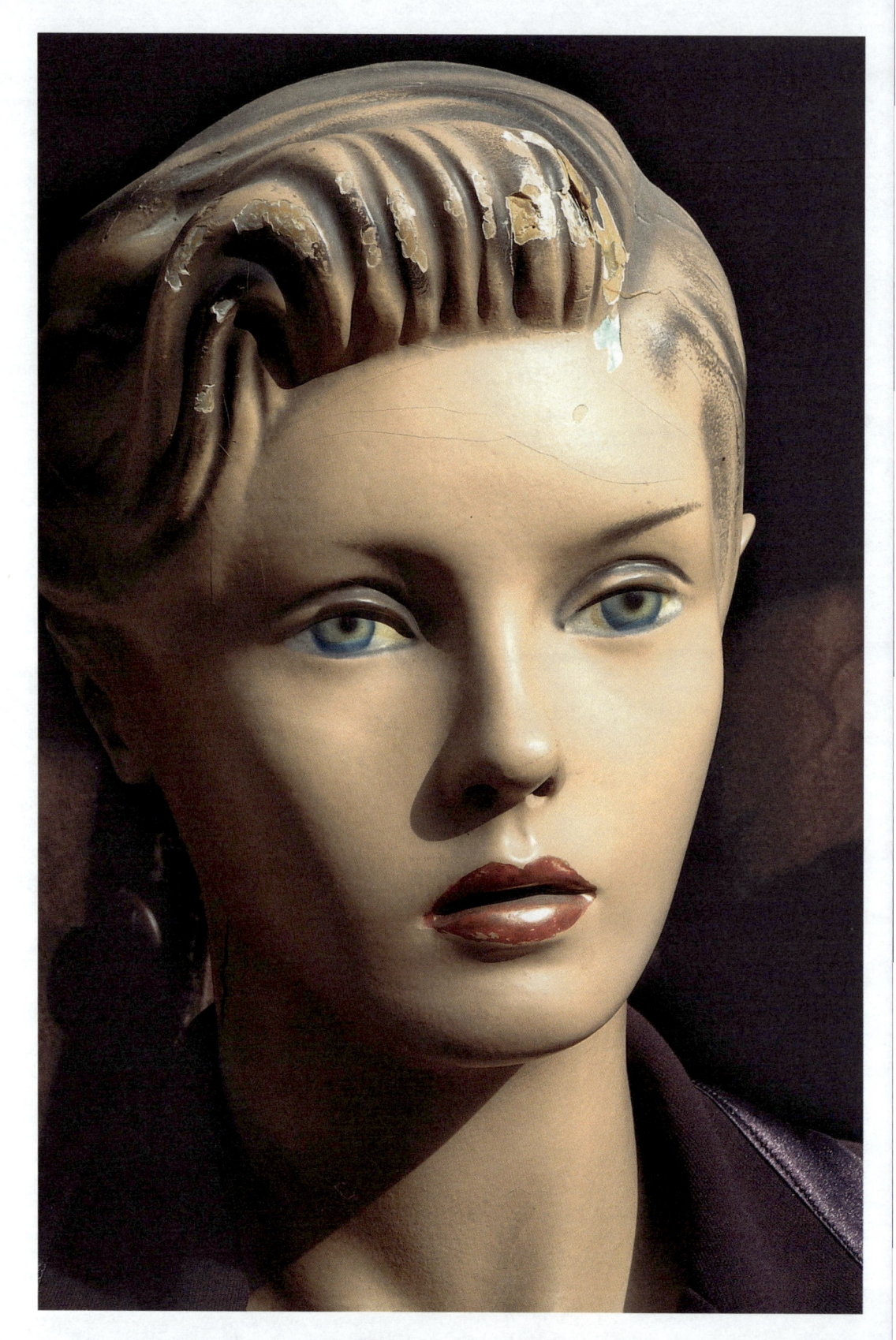

bantjes   marian

natasha kroll

In the period that Kroll worked at the Simpson shop, windows were of paramount importance to British retailers. Color print was prohibitively expensive in the U.K. until the early 1960s, so, while advertising remained a black-and-white informative affair, displays of actual merchandise were the primary vehicle for seducing customers. In her book *Window Display*, published in 1954, Kroll advised her fellow displaymen to "Forget the tricks of the trade." "Displays should not be labored," she advised; rather they should suggest "some degree of improvisation," although "great care and patience should have gone into producing this casual effect." Alongside photographs of her own arrangements and those of her peers, Kroll included images of ordinary hardware stores, greengrocers, and fishmongers. Her dislike of overbearing professionalism was matched by her love for the quotidian mastery of her craft.

In 1956 Kroll was recruited to the BBC by the head of the design department Richard Levin. Perhaps she had come to his attention after a particularly striking display. If not the daffodil heads, then it could have been the hat held on a pole with spectacles floating a few inches below, or the quirky glove-and-ball tree, or the set of suits and hats that, although unworn, appear to be enjoying a day at the races. Kroll spent a decade at the BBC before leaving to work freelance in film, including several collaborations with the director Ken Russell. She enjoyed great success in her post-Simpson career and in 1966 was one of the very few women to be appointed a Royal Designer for Industry. An article in the *Evening Standard* that appeared on the eve of her move from Simpson to the BBC hinted at the force behind Kroll's creative brilliance. "I pity the producer who has a passion for 'floral arrangements,'" it read. "If it doesn't suit Miss Kroll she'll be more inclined to substitute a crock of grasses and weeds gathered by the roadside. And I bet he won't have the nerve to move it."

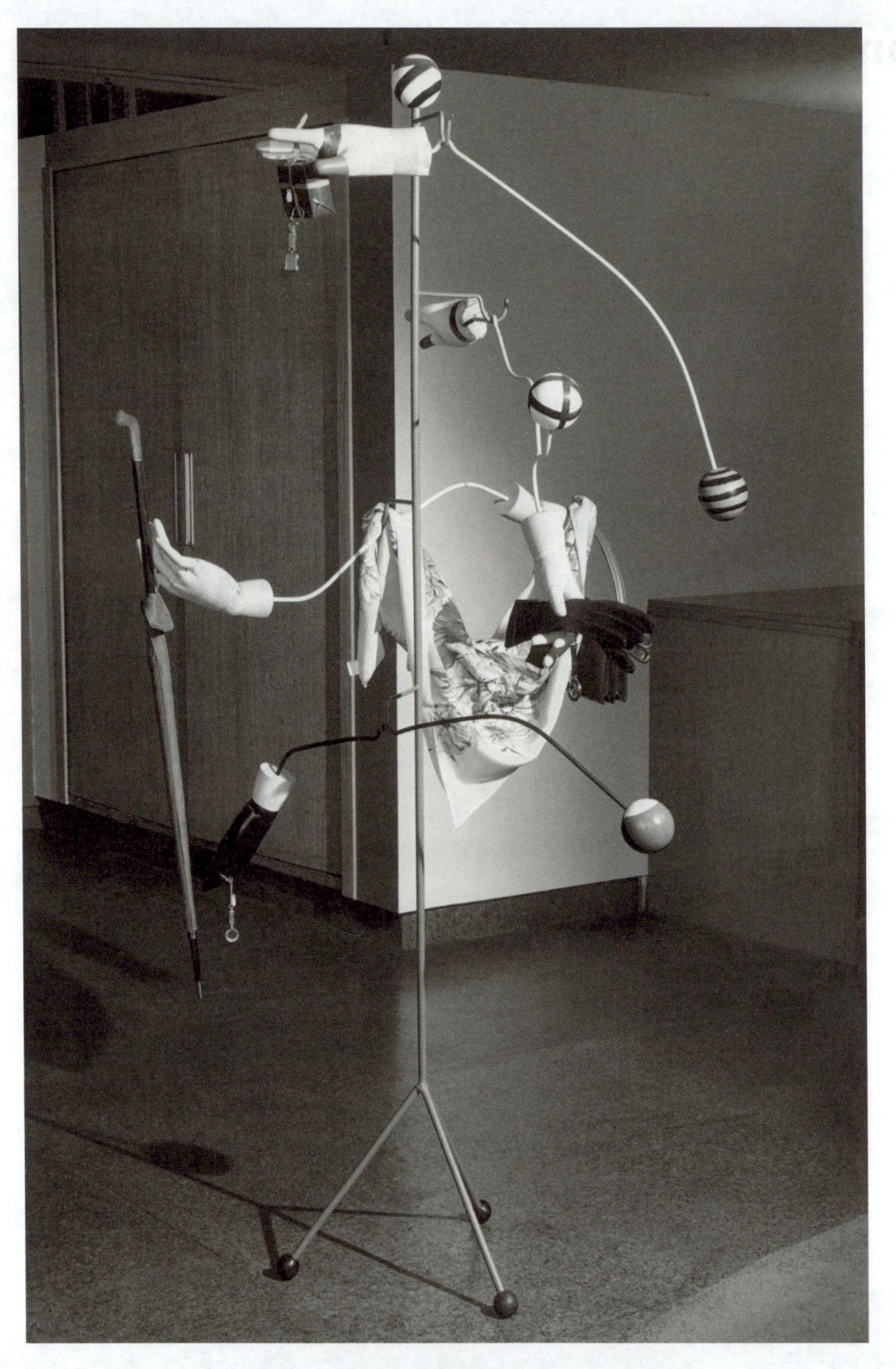

king   emily

Imagine the scene: London, March 1955; rationing in Britain ended last year, but scarcity remains the national condition. A man, perhaps he's wearing a heavy woolen overcoat, is walking along the south side of Piccadilly when a delightful tableau of domesticated surrealism grabs his attention. In the window of the clothing retailer Simpson there is a series of raincoats, invisibly suspended, but with the fabric positioned as if the coats are hurrying toward an important event. A large bunch of daffodils blooms from every collar. The sight of these flower men adds a spring to our protagonist's step. Perhaps it even tempts him to buy some new outerwear.

This arrangement was the creation of the shop's display manager Natasha Kroll, and while most Piccadilly habitués wouldn't have known her name, they would almost certainly have recognized her work. Employed by the store since 1942 (six years after it first opened in 1936), she and her team changed the windows weekly, and her style—merchandise matched with everyday props all arranged in a simple yet playful manner—had become a well-known feature of the thoroughfare. Within the trade Kroll was a confirmed celebrity. According to *Stores and Shops* magazine, she had "a flair and a talent which at times may be said to border on genius." "Her vision is fresh and penetrating and for all its application to sophisticated ends often has an almost naive quality, as rare among professional display men as it is welcome." After Kroll left Simpson, *Display* magazine even pondered, "Can a displayman be too good?" "What happens," it asked, "when the Krolls and Luckings depart [Eric Lucking was Kroll's counterpart at Liberty]? Can a display manager interpret a store's trading policy so brilliantly that he cannot be replaced?"

Born in Russia in 1914, Kroll and her family immigrated to Germany in the early 1920s. Kroll was educated in design at the Reimann-Schule in Berlin and then taught at the school until 1936, when she fled Nazi Germany along with her younger brother Alex Kroll. Arriving in London, Kroll became a teacher at the newly opened London branch of the Reimann and Alex, who later went on to work at the publisher Condé Nast, enrolled as a pupil. Kroll had strong links with European modernism, but, unlike fellow émigrés and occasional window-display designers László Moholy-Nagy and Serge Chermayeff, she also had sympathy for the Victoriana and folk art that were important ingredients of the postwar British aesthetic. "Her delight is to poke around junk shops where, for a song, she may pick up things such as the old wheelbarrow," reported *Stores and Shops*. And the *Evening Standard* newspaper celebrated her ability to "bring a midsummer madness to the most mundane things and give idiotic things a new sanity."

landscape stone

Appearing to be a painted panorama, a *pietra paesina*, or "landscape stone," is a natural anomaly. These stone renderings, composed deep underground millions of years ago, seem to depict landscapes of the terrestrial realm inhabited in much more recent history. The stones were created during the Cretaceous and Paleogene periods, between 145 and 23 million years ago, and are primarily made of calcareous clay limestone and petrified remains of marine organisms. Imagery appears in the stones wherever nature and chance collaborate, with human imagination completing the picture.

Masterful cutting of the stone also plays an important role in the pictorial effect: the specific orientation of the cut is key to revealing the latent images. In the 16th century, the Medici family acquired a quarry near Florence that was the source of a particularly beautiful stock of *pietra paesina*, and Cosimo de' Medici had slabs of the stone set into furniture and decorative objects. In the 16th and 17th centuries, these rock landscapes were disseminated throughout Europe, and Flemish painters in particular used them as lapidarian canvases on which they painted figures into the "naturalistic" scenes. Much later, in the 20th century, the visionary nature of the landscape stones coincided with the aberrant inclinations of the Surrealists, including André Breton himself, who wrote about the stones in his arts journal *Le Surréalisme, même*.

This specimen represents a certain variety of landscape stone known as "Florentine masurate" or "ruin marble," wherein rust-brown discolorations on a gray-blue background evoke ephemeral man-made structures such as castles, towers, and stone walls—all fallen into ruin.

de vera federico

sabon

I woke up one morning knowing however irrational and financially unrealistic it might seem in ordering a large shipment of custom cast lead type from a foreign country, some opportunities only a fool would pass up. The only way possible for me was to put it on the cuff and figure it out later. So I put in a custom line order specifying the quantities I wanted of each character, in multiple sizes, for the typeface Sabon. I chose the sizes 10 point, 12 point and 12-point small caps, and 24 point, to best suit the work I envisioned making once this type arrived in the States.

Four weeks later, after running around a couple airports and talking to customs officials, I picked up three meticulously packed wooden crates from a warehouse. Back at my studio with a close friend, opening the crates containing the type and spacing material, it felt as though we were pulling out the lost equation to the letterpress printing process. Someone once told me, "Different is different," and that sentence can't better explain the power and merit these tools possess compared to today's digital-influenced trends.

If one has the nerve to inquire, and somehow the bread to deliver, it is possible to get some of these amazing typefaces in multiple sizes, brand-spanking-new. But if one is serious, one must act fast, and put money where one's mouth is. One thing the letterpress resurgence did not bring with it was an army of young people looking to take over the dying and commercially unviable world of metal typecasting. As all of the experienced type castors like Mr. Gerstenberg, with decades of study, training, and experience get on in their years and retire or pass away, this amazing craft will soon diminish to static museum holdings—collecting dust, out of commission, and out of circulation. From this experience it has become clear to me that now is the time to act in developing a type collection that will take me through this century, and when I'm gone, hopefully take someone else into the next. I can't think of money better spent.

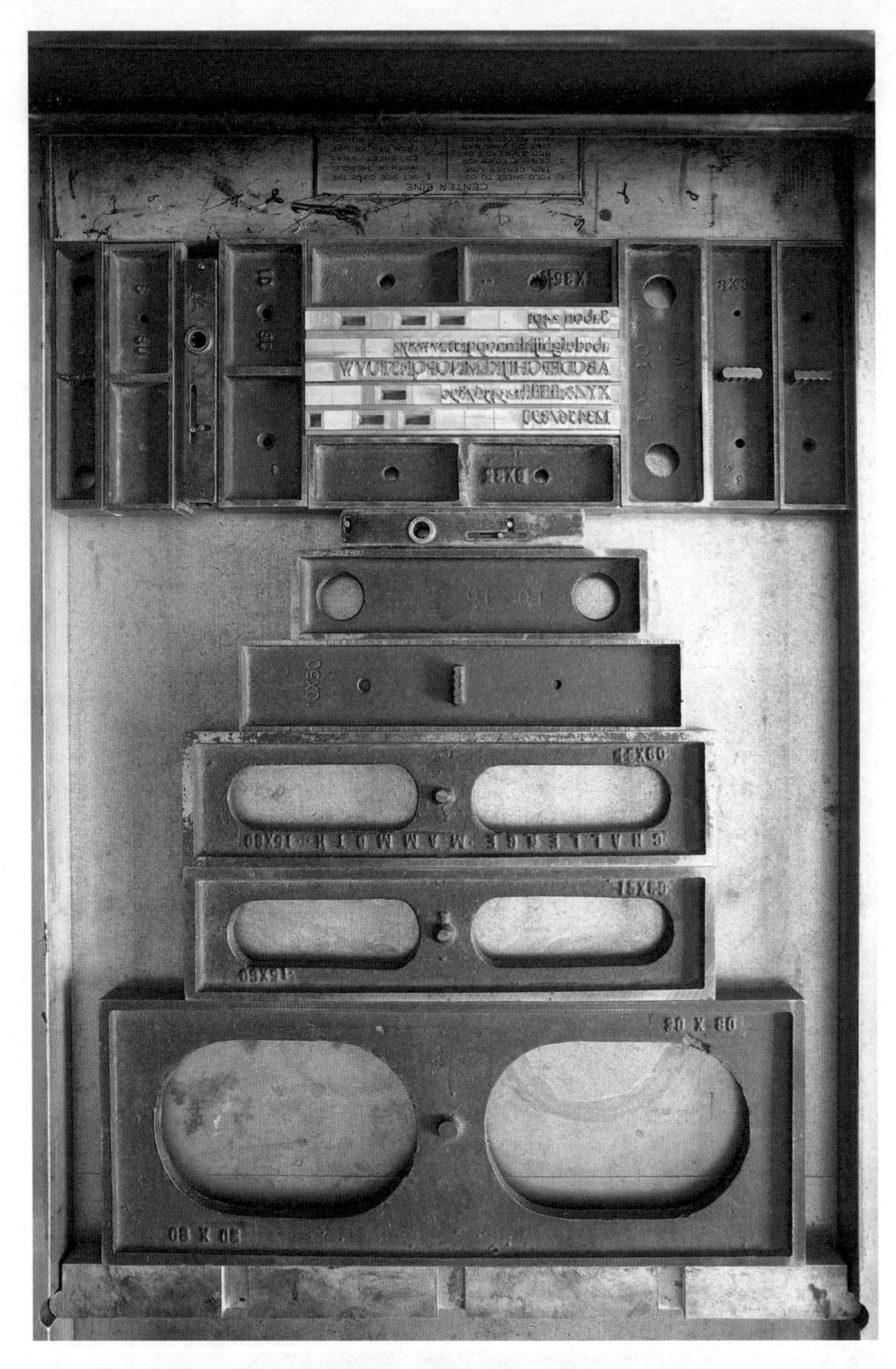

beacham jon

Over the past decade, a form of letterpress printing has seen a resurgence in America. But for a new generation of printers, working primarily with plates made from digital files, what was once a crucial element of not only good printing but also high-quality design has been almost completely ignored and forgotten —METAL TYPE.

In the early 1970s when photo-offset printing took hold as the new industry standard, print shops across the country began abandoning their letterpress machines and their type. A small number of fortunate printers from this era who were still dedicated to the craft of letterpress were able to score quality collections of type for pennies on the dollar before it was dumped, or hauled off to the scrap yard. Sadly, those days (and methods) of scoring type are long gone.

With only a few operating type foundries left in the world with the ability (and the matrices) to cast quality typefaces, the process of buying new type is more than challenging. Through research and word of mouth from others, I learned of Rainer Gerstenberg, who runs the foundry Druckerei R. Gerstenberg, located in Frankfurt, Germany. The foundry he operates has an amalgamation of type matrices from some of the best foundries formerly operating in Europe. (As most foundries slowly closed, some matrices for the most important type designs of the 20th century were saved and consolidated.)

One of the typefaces that Druckerei R. Gerstenberg is still capable of casting from original matrices is Sabon, designed by the famous typographer, book designer, and philosopher of such matters, Jan Tschichold. This typeface was a missing link in my shop, and well suited to the bookwork I am doing under my publishing imprint, The Brother in Elysium. My work requires having movable type in quantity in order to hand set a number of pages before having to print and redistribute type to begin setting new pages again.

blanc cassé

No one inhabits their interior more than a recluse, and the story of Wilsford Manor's aesthetic transmogrification is the story of its eccentric tenant's fifty years of staying in. It is a picture of an interior as palimpsest, of personality superseding style, and a domestic total work of art. Stephen Tennant was the archetypical consumptive—a published poet in his teens and ethereally beautiful. During the 1920s, he was the guiding spirit of the interwar phenomenon of the Bright Young People—a mostly aristocratic section of the "Lost Generation"—famous for their mania for novelty, parties, costume, tabloid notoriety, their characteristic hyperbolic shrieking speech adopted to rise above the giddy din of jazz bands and gramophones, their ironic Victoriana, and their ultramodernism. The hiccuping ebullience of those who came of age too late had an almost premonitory energy ahead of the next war to come, and Stephen, who seemed the most destined to expire, would outlive almost all of his contemporaries, sustained as a bedridden recluse, with Wilsford Manor his reliquary.

In 1930, at age twenty-four Stephen inherited Wilsford Manor, a 1906 Arts and Crafts–style house by Detmar Blow in Wiltshire, England. After divesting the place of its William Morris decor and other trappings of his mother's aristocratic bohemianism, an introduction from his own young society protégé, the photographer Cecil Beaton, led Stephen to the interior decorator Syrie Maugham. Middle-aged and recently divorced from her husband, the great gay novelist W. Somerset Maugham, Syrie was in her prime. Extravagant and energetic, she had not only invented her métier—decorating was then undertaken by firms without any pretensions to art, and it was not considered appropriate work for a woman—but had also succeeded in making her radical luxury style London's foremost choice.

Sharing a passionate fondness for seashells, Syrie and Stephen co-conceived a nautical iteration of Syrie's quintessential harmony of white on white. Her style, often called Vogue Regency, was a broadly expressed trumping of decorative over intrinsic value that increased in chic as the rooms grew to approximate stage sets. For Wilsford Manor: Venetian grotto furniture, nautical moldings of rope effect, side tables with legs of seahorse and barnacle motifs, waves of pearlescent satin draperies, and limed and whitewashed 19th-century pieces set amid the clean white walls of the spacious rooms.

Left in his gorgeous rooms, Stephen seemed to conform to his acquaintance Cyril Connolly's adage "Whom the gods wish to destroy they first call promising," alternating between deep languishing and fevered scheming; his unwritten novel, *Lascar: A Story of the Maritime Boulevards*, amounted to little more than exquisitely drawn frontispieces. As years passed, Stephen's exotic fascinations became lichen on Syrie's alabaster. Her chic white became a receptive support onto which a rococo of color and ornament was progressively heaped, making still lifes out of the interiors—nautilus, coral, fishnets, loggia and fountains, a reptile house, vast varieties of lilies (real and artificial), baskets of snowdrops, satins in all the hues of sunset, large straw hats (like ghosts from lost weekends) hung on the newel-posts of the staircase meant for the descending entrance, sketches by Beaton and Pavel Tchelitchew, French postcards and rose petals littering the skin rugs, ad infinitum: all creating the riot of arcana and paraphernalia of the self-imposed prisoner in his solitary glamour.

p. paul

wpa national park posters

Between 1935 and 1943 the Works Progress Administration's (WPA) Federal Art Project printed over two million posters in thirty-five thousand different designs to excite public interest in education, theater, health, safety, and travel. The early posters were hand painted and produced in limited quantities. After implementation of improved screen-printing processes, the artistic complexity of the posters grew and larger editions were made possible at a relatively low cost. Today, only two thousand known examples survive.

In 1938, the WPA extended its program to the National Park Service, and posters were printed and distributed to encourage park visitation. At the close of the program in 1941, the remnants were mothballed by the parks, only to be forgotten for decades. In 1973, a Grand Teton National Park poster destined for the burn pile aroused the curiosity of park ranger Doug Leen. This marked the start of a quest for the lost park posters that continues to this day.

In the early 1990s, thirteen black-and-white negatives of posters surfaced within the National Park Service archives. This led Ranger Doug to re-edition the original park posters, which were now in the public domain. Since only fourteen parks had subscribed to the WPA poster program, many parks today have commissioned Ranger Doug and his collaborator Brian Maebius to create contemporary designs in the historical style. While respecting the original designs, Ranger Doug takes subtle creative liberties such as introducing new elements like cars and human figures to emphasize the monumental scale of the parks. When information is missing, Ranger Doug and Maebius glean elements from historic park brochures and printed matter such as era-specific colors and details.

Amusingly, the crude character of the original WPA posters would be considered "bad printing" by today's image standards. Yet their elemental charm has caught the attention of the National Park Service and park goers alike. With new discoveries of originals, and new designs underway, Ranger Doug continues to uncover the beautiful bold and graphic work of the WPA era.

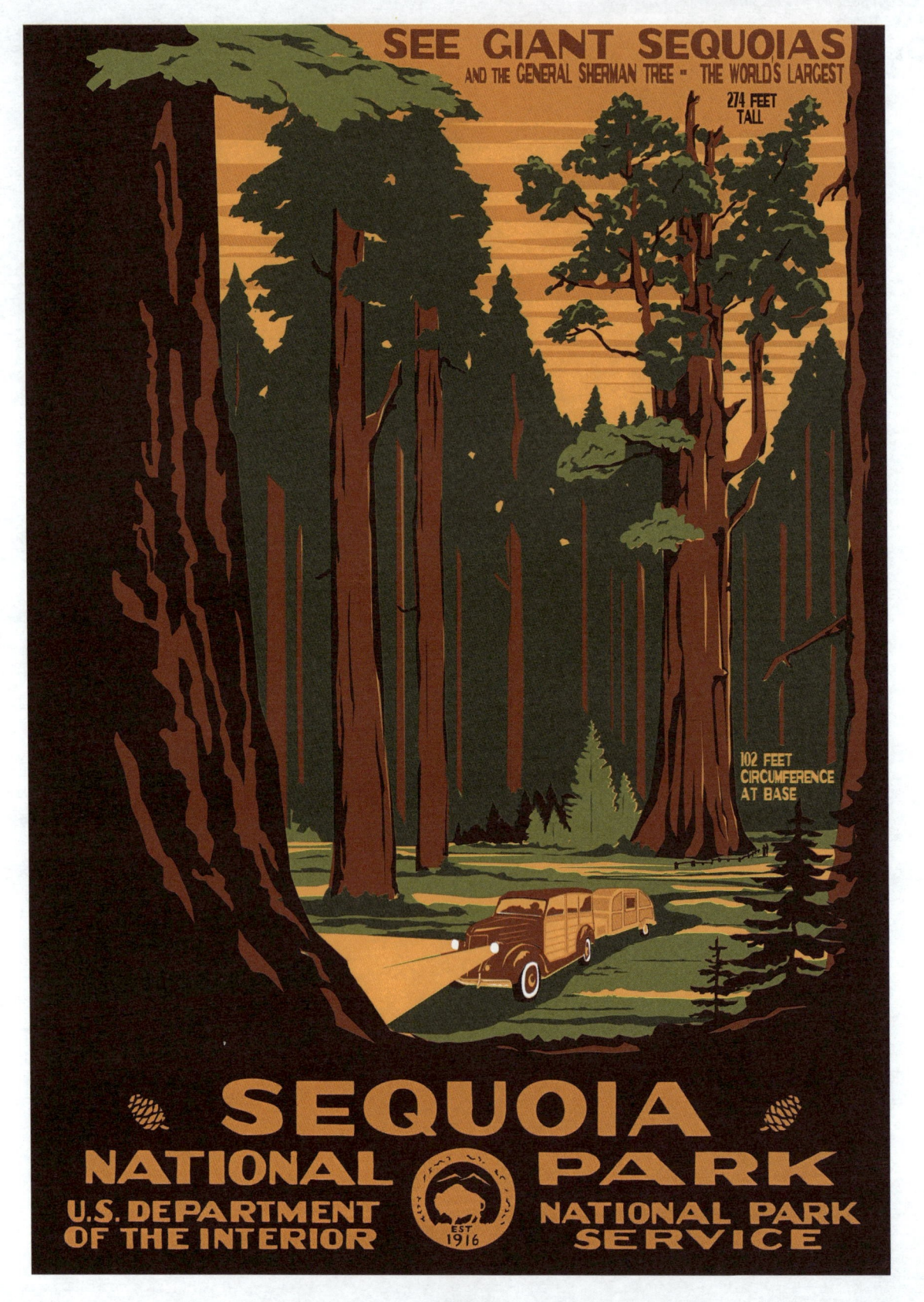

Doug Leen and Brian Maebius. *General Grant*, 2009. (left) and *Sequoia*, 2007. (right)

liemburg harmen

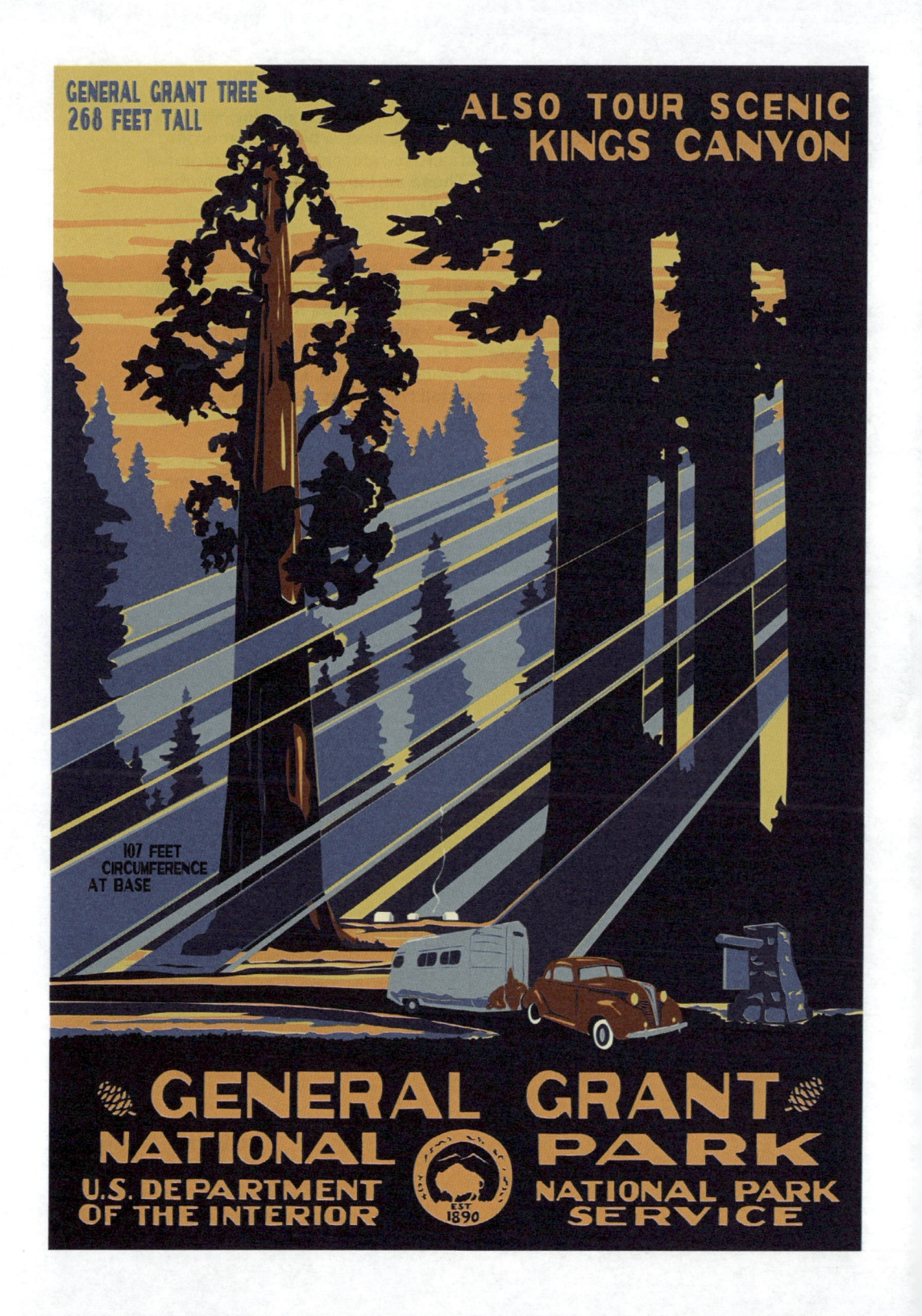

big map

As a book designer, I like to juxtapose information on opposing pages. The space between the pages, across the fold, is where the story is told. This technique is especially effective as a narrative device when designing atlases. An aerial photograph on one page with a map on the next, a historic recording followed by a future projection, statistical data cross-referenced with a regional map—here is where the story of time is told. These various kinds of information graphics challenge each other—and us, the reader—about what the true representation of a city is.

Through my experience in map making, I have come to realize that it is difficult to tell a story with a single map. And it was exactly this challenge that I was asked to do this past year, to design a single map of Belgium for the Belgian Pavilion at the Venice Architecture Biennale. I intended to show that the country is not a network of cities but a continuous "soup" of functions where residential areas, agriculture, industry, and nature coexist and blend. In the end, I used scale as a means to give the map two faces, to let the map tell two stories: one from a distance and one from up close.

The map I made for the Belgian Pavilion was big. At fifteen meters by four meters (fifty feet by thirteen feet), it is by far the biggest map I have ever made. The map was created using geographic information systems (GIS) data projected on a fifty-by-fifty-meter (164-by-164-foot) grid to a 1:2,000 scale. From a distance, where the grid is visible and clear, pixels emerge—the map appears digital. When examined closer, one sees that the legend of the map consists of axonometric drawings, and so the map feels almost handmade. The pixels dissolve into a hand-drawn landscape. Data becomes reality.

Joost Grootens. *A Land Never* (detail), 2012.

grootens   **joost**

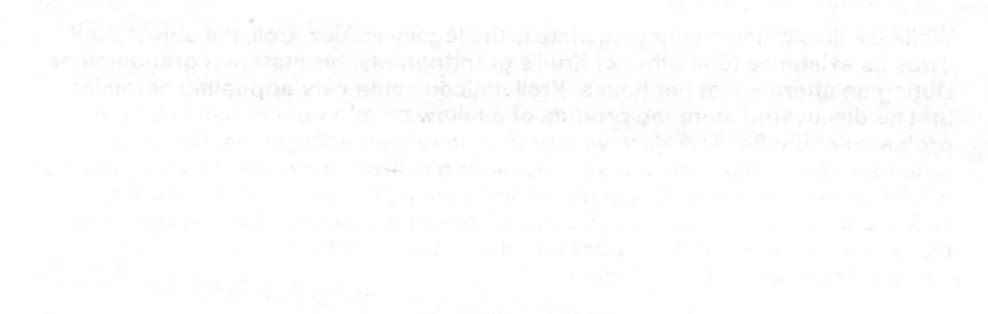

denim and clay

While the illustration on the stag plate is the legacy of Alex Kroll, the object itself owes its existence to another of Kroll's grandparents, his maternal grandmother. During an afternoon at her house, Kroll noticed some very appealing ceramics that he discovered were the product of a fellow member of her local choir. A professor of English literature who prefers to remain anonymous, this amateur potter agreed to make some pieces according to Kroll's designs. It was a process of trial and error—Kroll's first suggestions were totally unsuited to the potter's skills—but eventually they arrived at the plates. Kroll learned a huge amount about clay in the process and the potter had the opportunity to demonstrate his extraordinary talent for freehand illustration.

Kroll's fascination for jeans lies in the transparency of their construction—their selvedge seams and patch pockets—and related interests have taken him into territories beyond denim. Kroll's non-clothing range includes a pair of cast brass dice, a cow-horn comb, and an unusually real bearlike sheepskin teddy bear. As with the plates, each of these things was made by a craftsman who, with Kroll's encouragement, took well-honed skills into new territories. In some cases this has caused pain—the amateur soft-toy maker sewing the fleece bears ended up with very sore fingers as such toys are usually made with fabrics with more give. But even suffering has led to invention, such as a toy in the form of a humpback whale made of relatively easy-to-sew cotton dyed with Mexican logwood. Although this whale has no direct connection with either of Kroll's grandparents, it is in the same lineage as the plates. The shape was the suggestion of Kroll's wife, Deborah, and, in part, it came from tailoring demands to suit available skills. It is the product of family wisdom, curiosity, and a willingness to adapt—all qualities that are at the heart of Kroll's projects.

king emily

William Kroll is best known as a small-batch jeans maker. After working for the Japanese brand Evisu, he started his own label, Tender Co., in 2009. He is celebrated among denim fetishists for his use of natural dyes such as purple logwood and woad as well as his elegantly honest approach to construction. Kroll's core business is tiny but is going strong; yet, when asked about products that represent his current activity, rather than showing me a pair of trousers, he went to his stock (which he keeps at home) and ferreted out a hand-thrown clay plate.

Around eleven inches in diameter, it is made of red clay slipped with white. At its center is an illustration of a stag created using a technique called sgraffito, which involves scratching through the upper layer of white clay to the dark red clay beneath—Roman frescos were made this way. The drawing consists of a single yet incredibly elaborate line, with the stag's body built of gestures suggestive of ampersands and its antlers loop edged. The plate is one of a set of three, all slightly different in size and each illustrated in the same style, the second showing a robin in flight and the third the head of a satyr with modest crescent-moon horns.

All three emblems are examples of early 18th-century German engraving taken from Jan Tschichold's marvelous book *Schatzkammer der Schreibkunst*. First published in Switzerland in 1945, with an English version produced in 1966 under the title *Treasury of Alphabets and Lettering*, this volume contains page after page of exquisite examples of decorative lettering. Kroll's copy is a rare German-language original that he inherited along with several other enviable books from the library of his grandfather, the art director and editor Alex Kroll. Kroll enjoyed an unusually close relationship with his grandfather. As a child he would travel from his family home in Oxford to Alex Kroll's house on Fulham Road to spend time together visiting art galleries and absorbing the older man's milieu. Later, when he was studying menswear at Central Saint Martins College of Art and Design, Kroll lived in the basement of that same house. Alex Kroll was a German émigré of Russian-Jewish origin and his circle included significant figures in London's postwar cultural life, such as the gallerist Annely Juda and the graphic designer Germano Facetti. Kroll remembers that during the period they lived together, his grandfather took a newspaper every day but changed his subscription regularly. Looking at the world through the lens of the *Guardian* one day and that of the *Telegraph* the next, he never allowed his point of view to ossify.

sol rosen

In 1933, as America struggled through the depths of the Great Depression, a young man named Sol Rosen joined Maharam's fledgling Chicago sales force. Maharam was just entering its fourth decade in business and was in the process of expanding from its original location on West 46th Street in New York's theater district to Chicago, St. Louis, and eventually Los Angeles. Under the leadership of Joe, Arthur, Mac, and Sam Maharam, the company morphed from a peddler of fabric remnants into the "style authority for costume and stage decoration."

Though it paid only twelve dollars a week, Sol's first job was worth much more to this exuberant eighteen-year-old, offering a backstage pass to a vivid world of vaudeville and burlesque theater, dance schools, nightclubs, and traveling circuses. It even granted him entrée into the dressing room of Olympic gold medalist and ice-review star Sonja Henie, who demanded a special shade of transparent peach velvet for her toilette, delivered by Sol personally. At the end of his first week, this self-described "virtual dynamo," who ran everywhere rather than waste time walking, came home exhausted and slept fourteen hours straight.

During this era of the postage stamp, Sol Rosen's business correspondence with Joe Maharam, or "J.M.," was comprehensive and stretched from July 1938 until December 1945. It paints a picture of an ambitious young man whose ceaseless desire to improve his station in life mirrored the nation's efforts to rebuild in the wake of economic collapse.

Early on, before he was entrusted with the keys to his boss's Chevrolet, Sol would make his deliveries by hitching a ride on the back of an obliging truck, pocketing his fourteen-cent streetcar fare. While his hopeless scheming occasionally landed him in hot water—in one letter, J.M. accuses him of "doping out a different proposition" "every other Sunday and Thursday"—more often than not, Sol's relentless, resourceful nature made him an invaluable employee—a veritable "Kid Dynamite"—to a company on the move. Charting a young man's course through life's early milestones—a wedding (a "ball and chain festival"), quickly followed by a baby (a real "humdinger") and voluntary service in the Army Air Forces during World War II (which was hoped to last only a year thanks to "the help of the good old Russian boys")—these letters, with their colorful sprinkling of ostrich feathers and gold sequins, are a treasure.

sheth sara

MAHARAM FABRIC CORPORATION

INTER-OFFICE COMMUNICATION

DATE July 20, 1938.

Sol ──────
c/o ──────
St. Lou──,

Dear Nephew Solly,

This is to acknowledge your beautifully written letter of the 19th and I am not sarcastic when I say this. You can rest assured that I realize what you are up against in St. Louis and I feel you are quite equal to the situation. There is no reason why we shouldn't get our share of the business if we cooperate with you which we will do to our best ability.

<u>EDISON BROS. OMBRE TRIPLEX</u> - We can have these goods made in the ombre effect for 32½¢. It won't be the best job in the world as the fellow who does the Ombre cannot do a perfect job. However, we have sold the Ombre work to Edison that this chap turned out and they never kicked.

<u>OMBRE GEORGETTE</u> - We can turn out a 39" Rayon Ombre Georgette at a cost of 25¢. I figured it as close as I could and think you should be able to get this order. I would quote at least 31¢ for the Ombre Georgette and 38½¢ for the Ombre Triplex. You are on the ground so use your own judgement.

<u>18" SEQUIN CLOTH</u> - I think we will be out of the picture on this thing because of the fact that we have sold all our goods here and would have to pick it up from a jobber. They want $4.50 per yard for the 18" and it wouldn't pay to sell it for less than $5.00 per yard. Ours is a 65 row Sequin which we will enclose sample of.

<u>BADER</u> - Art Maharam will write you on the Chromeflex today.

<u>MATHES</u> - "   "   "   "   "   "   " Colorej Art Board.

I am having samples mailed parcel post to you on the Ombre Triplex and Ombre Georgette. I may mention that Ombre Triplex work may not be as nice as the sample but it will be the same effect. I think it best not to tell them anything.

Another suggestion you can make would be our Ombre Panne Satin. I have no sample of this . This would give them a soft effect and would cost us 25¢ per yard. You can show them the cloth and maybe they can visualize it.

I am writing all your letters in duplicate to Phil so that he has any further ideas other than mine he can get in touch with you.

Love and kisses,

Uncle Joe

JF:HB

sissinghurst

In the gardens of Sissinghurst Castle in England, there are places to sit and rest. Or Read. Or Reflect.

After sitting, it is good to stroll through the gardens.

There is a great amount of design Everywhere, but best not to speak of that right NOW. For NOW, we can just exist in a pleasant, undemanding state, listening to the birds sing.

kalman   **maira**

g. lorenzi

By the late 1950s, Giovanni and Lina had retired to the mountains, and ceded responsibility for the store to their sons, who had started working there by sweeping floors and cleaning shelves. One son, Franco, was a talented salesman, while Aldo had a flair for craftsmanship, devoting much of his time to finding suitable products and liaising with their makers. He and his wife, Edda, often spent their holidays searching for suppliers. Aldo once returned triumphantly from sailing in Tenerife having spotted a source of cord key rings.

Over the years, the store was enlarged, and new merchandise introduced. Still billed as a *coltellinaio*, or cutlery shop, it also stocked smoking supplies, toiletries, and kitchen tools among its eighteen thousand products, as well as displaying antique knives, scissors, and razors in a small museum. "I love the articles that I sell," wrote Aldo in his 2008 book *That Shop in Via Montenapoleone*. "I sell them hoping that whoever buys them will use them, cherish them, and keep them for as long as possible."

Everything was lovingly presented in gleaming wooden cabinets or copper-framed windows, and packaged exquisitely. If you were looking for, say, a cheese knife, you would be shown dozens of subtly different ones, each particularly well suited to a specific cheese. The staff were instructed to be equally attentive to every customer, regardless of how much money they spent. The same meritocratic spirit applied to the merchandise. Popular brands of soap were displayed alongside exquisite handmade combs and brushes on the basis that they were all exemplars of their respective types.

When Giovanni arrived on via Montenapoleone, the street was filled with specialist traders. One by one, they have closed, replaced by the same global luxury brands you see on expensive shopping streets the world over. After the same fate befell G. Lorenzi, Milan was left a little blingier, yet much poorer.

rawsthorn

alice

Whenever I go to Milan there are certain things I love to do: peering across the city from the Duomo roof, eating at Latteria, and browsing around Achille Castiglioni's design studio. I cannot always squeeze them all into the same visit, but I have always managed to find time for one Milanese ritual—shopping at the beautiful G. Lorenzi cutlery store on via Montenapoleone.

Not anymore. After years of selling and repairing knives, scissors, brushes, razors, and thousands of other useful, impeccably crafted objects on the corner of via Montenapoleone and via Pietro Verri, the Lorenzi family sold the store.

Its demise robbed Milan of not only one of its most intriguing stores, but also a memento of the artisanal heritage that fueled Italy's industrial success in the 20th century and the country's *gioia di vivere*, or joyful spirit, before it was scarred by the credit crunch and "bunga bunga" politics.

The Lorenzis were in the knife trade long before the store's founder, Giovanni Lorenzi, was born in 1899 in Mortaso, a small village in the mountainous Trentino region of northern Italy. Like most of their neighbors, they farmed in summer and spent the winter traveling farther afield to earn extra money by sharpening knives on portable grinding wheels. When Giovanni was in his teens, he and his brother Olimpio were apprenticed to a knife grinder in Germany. In 1919, they moved to Milan and rented premises on Corso Magenta. Ten years later, Giovanni opened his own store on via Montenapoleone.

Helped by his wife, Lina, he sold knives and scissors on the first floor and repaired them on a grinding wheel in the basement. Soon they established a network of skilled artisans, each specializing in a particular material or technique, and commissioned them to make objects to their specifications, often using wood, horn, leather, copper, and other traditional rustic materials. The same wealth of artisanal skills would prove indispensable to Italy's furniture makers in the postwar era, and later to its fashion designers.

one good thing

I met Andrée Putman when I was in my twenties during my first chapter at Maharam. She was riding the immediate fame that followed the opening of the Morgans Hotel, the project that made her an icon. I had the idea that she might lend her talent to designing modest textiles, as she had to that modest hotel property. She declined. Over the years we became friendly, and when I returned to run Maharam in 1997 she offered to assist in the reinvention of the company. I explained that our stage was so poorly set that any effort was sure to fall flat. She countered with the idea that we might get started by developing an affordable synthetic horsehair for a collection of luggage she was designing. We ended up liking the textile so much that we were inspired to adapt it for seating, and thus she became Maharam's first de facto collaborator, paving the way for more intensely focused collaborations to come.

Memorably, Andrée and I were walking to lunch at the Oyster Bar at Grand Central Station one day, and along the way we were amused by a shop window brimming with the sort of faux cinematic baubles typically featured on television shopping networks. Andrée dragged me into the shop and—in her uniquely sonorous baritone—insisted that we were obliged to find "just one good thing." The fact that she felt that one good thing could be found in this gilt treasure chest amazed me, but after a few moments, she succeeded in her unceasingly stylish way, and a valuable lesson was taken in the unlikely origin of beauty and the substance instilled in an object through authoritative interpretation. Andrée lives on, through this and the many lessons she shared with me and all those who knew her and admired her work.

Pierre et Gilles. *Andrée Putman*, 1982.

maharam   **michael**

avifauna

I am intrigued by the dynamic interchange between design, technique, and material. A good example of this relationship is the work of Dutch designers Maarten Kolk and Guus Kusters, whose projects balance nature and culture, emphasizing the beauty of both worlds.

With *Avifauna*, Kolk and Kusters have invented a playful form of taxidermy, resulting in a series of taxidermied birds that replaces feathers with molded textiles. Starting with the skeletons of various specimens (all have died of natural causes), the designers reconstituted the form of each bird with a man-made material, using the outer textile layer to reflect the character of the species: a wood owl is cloaked in thick, brown wool felt; painted linen defines the elegant gray heron; a seagull is somehow appropriately wrapped in disposable polyfoam. The birds remain intact, each having been given personalized coats—a second skin as well as a second life. I think that if a bird could dress itself, it would wear these garments.

eyck   thomas

the swan

I shot this photograph at the Edna Lawrence Nature Lab—a miniature and highly concentrated natural history museum designed specifically for learning on the Rhode Island School of Design campus. Within the Nature Lab are thousands of animal, plant, and mineral specimens used as resources for young artists to draw from real life—instead of just Googling low-quality images off the web.

For instance, this photograph of a swan doesn't do the great swan justice by any means. But when you stand in front of it, you feel its presence and majesty. As you walk around it and stare closely at it, you see every subtlety that would otherwise be lost. And why is it under glass? Because the other beautiful swan that is propped up just a few feet away from this one—not under glass—looks as if it's served time as a chimney sweep. The soot-like dust that covers it doesn't come from the chimneys, of course, but instead from the charcoal RISD freshmen use in voluminous quantities to render their hand-drawn images. On some evenings when I peered into the Nature Lab to see the freshmen drawing, it felt a bit like watching the old *Peanuts* cartoons with Pig-Pen's wondrous cloud of dust following him everywhere he goes. Charcoal dust was literally everywhere—hitting RISD's bear (yes, the college has a bear), marlin, and a variety of specimens in "the wild" of the Nature Lab—everyone except this perfectly white swan, a symbol of serenity and purity, just like nature would want it to be. Untaxidermied, of course, but hey, the world isn't perfect.

maeda   **john**

le thoronet

It was the late Bruce Chatwin who told me I should visit the 12th-century Cistercian abbey of Le Thoronet, in Provence, and it has been years since I first made the journey. The setting is breathtaking—encircling hills, a densely forested valley with a river running through it—but the abbey itself is the object of the journey: a sublime example of what happens when architecture is shaped by simplicity. I always come away feeling that the clarity of my senses has been restored. Even though I am generally quite an impatient person, at Le Thoronet I am happy to sit in one place all day, just watching the way the sun moves around the building, enjoying the quality of the spaces and the atmosphere.

I remember taking my elder son to Le Thoronet one summer holiday. He must have been four or five years old and he began running up and down one of the benches in the church. An elderly tourist told him to be quiet, but a priest who was there admonished the man, saying that the boy should be allowed to be himself. I think the priest understood that as a child you express the excitement of that space physically. I put on an exhibition there called *Leçons du Thoronet* (which later became a book) to try and explain the impact the place has had on my approach to architecture. The expression of joy from such architecture is a key lesson.

pawson   **john**

the elemental egg

When I was a boy, the most fascinating place I knew was my father's desk drawer—it was filled with the most unimaginable, exotic treasures. Among all the strange and unidentifiable objects, I fixated on a peculiarly shaped silver egg that had the most appealing weight and density. Years later, as a thieving teen, I made off with my treasure . . . luckily my father never found me out. It wasn't until my early twenties that I came to learn the story of this coveted object and to acknowledge the egg as my earliest awareness of the elemental nature of things, which would come to define my aesthetic ideal. The super egg was popularized in the mid-1960s by Danish poet and scientist Piet Hein, who saw the potential of the superellipse shape in its unique combination of rectangle and circle. Hein advocated the use of the superellipse in city planning, furniture, and housewares. Early examples include a silver vessel produced by Georg Jensen, a liquid-filled silver "ice cube," and a satisfyingly dense brass fetish object sold with a random array of leather satchels. The super egg is still in production today, though in rather soulless stainless steel and glass.

maharam **michael**

wild swimming

Early in the evening, the best time of the day, I shake off life's cares by going for a wild swim. Wild swimming, as in a lake, is nothing like swimming in a pool. Apart from any other occasional wild swimmer, I am alone in the water. I am aware of any fellow swimmers, but time and again I feel as though the water belongs to me and nobody else.

At this time of day the last rays of evening sunlight have a silvery splendor as they fall on the crowns of trees, and sometimes on the water too. There is hardly a breath of wind, and even the air above the water is motionless. All I hear are my own movements as my arms hit the water, churning up waves on its surface, and then the reverberations as the waves fade away in the distance.

There's something ominous about the unknown depths beneath me, but they make me feel part of something bigger, connected to the animals and plants I imagine are down there. As the concerns of daily life disappear from my thoughts, I become one with the elements. Filling every pore is a sense of gratitude for my existence.

My favorite stroke is the breaststroke, which is not a very sporty stroke. It is more of a smoothly gliding movement through the water. Every sweep of the arms sets off a concert of softly splashing musical notes. I alternate the breaststroke with the backstroke, in which my arms rotate steadily as the clouds overhead point me in the right direction. My ears sink below the surface, eliminating every sound, and all I feel is the world gliding by beneath me.

Swimming has always been part of my life. Much of my youth was spent living close to a tributary that feeds into the Rhine River. At first my mother didn't allow my brothers or me to swim in the river for fear of the rats in the water, although later we owned a small boat that we mostly used for swimming parties.

When I was young we never went on vacation. Instead, my summers consisted of a season ticket to the village swimming pool, to which I cycled every morning with twenty-five cents in my pocket. As my girlfriends were on vacation, I often spent whole summers there with little company, apart from one of my brothers. Boredom was never a danger at the pool, for there were always new tricks to learn on one of the diving boards. Or I would create the biggest possible splash to catch the eye of the only nice boy from the village. A mixture of exhilarating freedom and total languidness fill my memories.

When I was about thirty I swam for a while with a monofin, a big fin attached to both feet that makes you look like a mermaid and lets you to propel yourself forward rapidly. The speed and nature of the movements gave me an animalistic sensation, as if I were a dolphin. Wearing a snorkel as well as a monofin meant I could stay underwater for longer. The feeling was meditative—far from the world, gravity suspended, no sound at all, no images.

Now, though, I only swim under my own power, unassisted by tools. For the first few yards I keep my head dry, until the cold shivers stop running down my arms and legs. As soon as the water feels pleasant, I take the plunge, dip my head beneath the surface, and really start to swim.

Every single time, I have to force myself to jump into the cold water. The discipline required is comparable to that needed when starting out on a creative process: mild anxiety beforehand, the dread of hardships ahead, the will to persevere and get the job done. Yet also the reward of tingling arms and legs, clear sensations, and a mind cleansed.

jongerius

hella

hans christian andersen's paper cuts

Many people are familiar with stories like "The Little Mermaid," "The Princess and the Pea," and "The Steadfast Tin Soldier." Fewer people know that their author, the Danish fairy-tale writer and poet Hans Christian Andersen, also had a talent for the visual arts.

Throughout his life Andersen made numerous drawings and no fewer than one thousand paper cuts. Although his imaginative, expressive, and sometimes bizarre cutouts enjoyed a host of admirers in his lifetime, he himself regarded creating them as an unpretentious pastime. Later on in life, when his success as a writer gained momentum, Andersen was the darling of the European royalty, entertaining his hosts by reading stories. On these occasions, he often wielded—according to several accounts—his enormous pair of scissors, cutting improvised party decorations to his guests' astonishment and pleasure.

The paper cuts were often based around a single fold in the paper, providing a vertical axis for the shape to come. Strategic cuts around this axis—in effect, drawing with the scissors—yielded a symmetrical form when the paper was unfolded. This technique was often used to create figures and heads.

Throughout the years, Anderson's visual work reflected his dramatic private iconography that was heavily influenced by a strong love for the theater: cupids, a hanged man, a dancer, hearts, and trees. A year before his death, a skull was added to this array.

Hans Christian Andersen. *Circle with Acrobats and Dansers*, 1859.

158

liemburg   **harmen**

anni albers: hardware

In 1940, renowned Bauhaus weaver Anni Albers and student Alex Reed created a collection of jewelry from basic household items. They sourced materials from hardware stores and five-and-dime shops such as paper clips, bobby pins, erasers, wine corks, metal sieves, washers, and nuts. By utilizing these objects decoratively and formally, Albers and Reed created a collection of anti-luxury jewelry that proposed a new definition of value.

Albers and Reed first met at Black Mountain College, the legendary experimental art school located in the Great Smoky Mountains of North Carolina. The school offered a progressive liberal arts education that fueled the American avant-garde from 1933 to 1956. Collaborations between teachers, students, and visiting artists were encouraged and, accordingly, Albers and Reed worked and traveled together.

It was during their trip to Oaxaca, Mexico, that they encountered the pre-Columbian jewelry of Monte Albán. The thousand-year-old jewelry was composed of unusual material combinations of precious and non-precious elements—pearls and seashells, rock crystals and gold. To Albers and Reed, this jewelry offered an insight into the wisdom of material value.

Albers and Reed's collection was borne from this logic. They were able to approach material as elemental form, dissociated from its prior purpose. Later associations of industrial hardware as ornament can be found in the punk fashions of the 1970s and '80s. But rather than seeking to subvert the status quo, the jewelry designs of Albers and Reed had their humble beginnings in the ancient relics of Monte Albán—creating a collection that affirmed ancient aesthetics through forward-focused practicality.

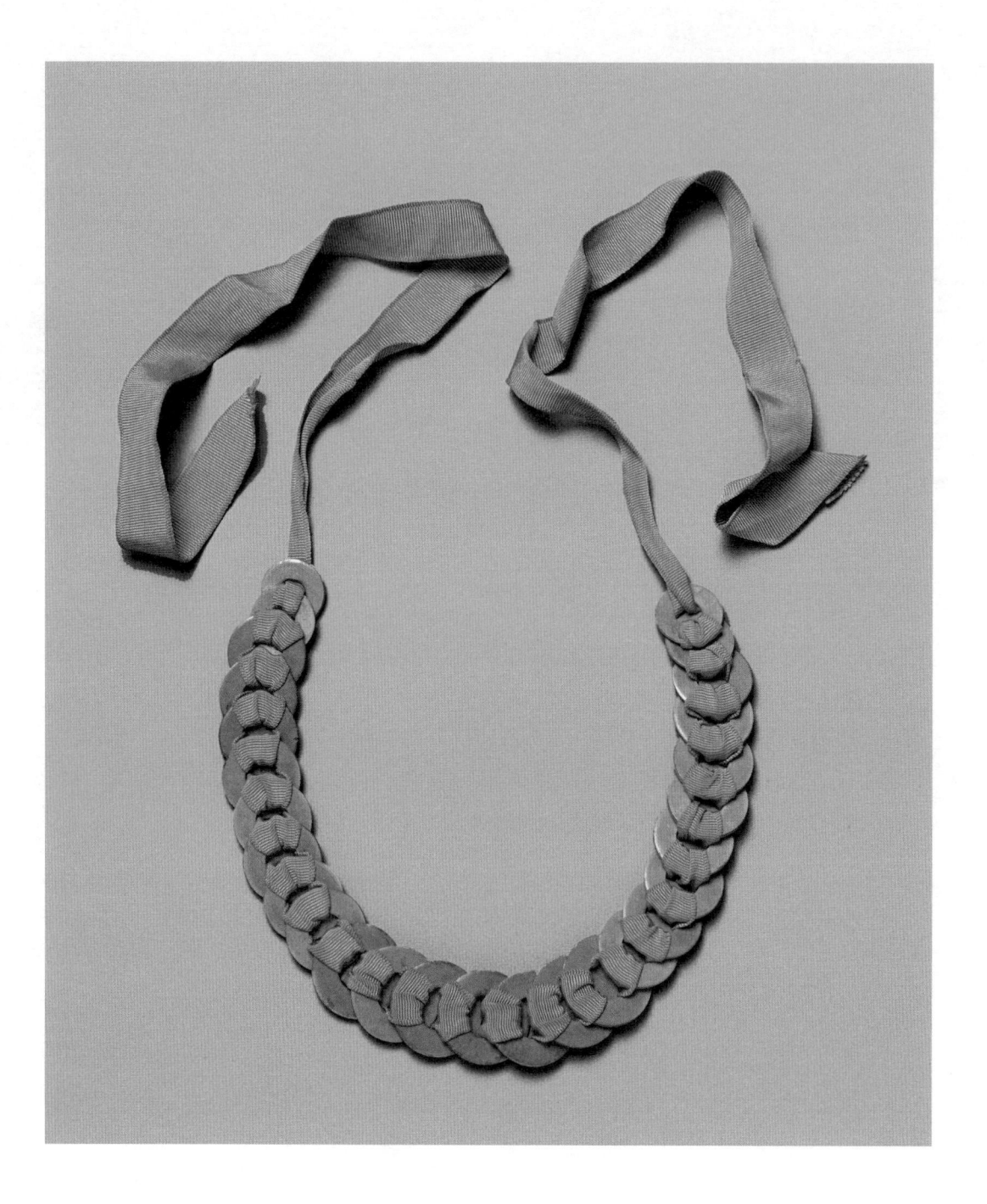

Anni Albers. Necklace, ca. 1940.

salisbury **bailey**

pale light:
samuel beckett & painting

In the final moments of the first act, Beckett's stage directions for *Waiting for Godot* asks for light that "*. . . suddenly fails. In a moment it is night. The moon rises at back, mounts in the sky, stands still, shedding a pale light on the scene.*" In the next direction Estragon is to "*contemplate the moon.*" Here, Estragon utters the line, "Pale for weariness." Broken by Vladimir's "Eh?," Estragon finishes, "Of climbing heaven and gazing on the likes of us." This is the very passage marked "K.D. Friedrich" in Beckett's notebook from the play, revealing the exact painting Beckett had in mind when he wrote the scene.

As Knowlson points out in the survey *Images of Beckett*, Caspar David Friedrich's painting might have only been referenced as an ironic nod toward the narratives of Christianity that Beckett was familiar with but had personally abandoned. And yet Beckett remained throughout his life a serene spirit, in many ways an artist highly concerned with the nature of being and, of course, our relationship with language. In my mind, this is where the role of painting most clearly came in handy to Beckett the writer: to alleviate the anxiety so many words induce in our consciousness, the stillness of paintings and their silences offered Beckett an obvious retreat. In that direction, toward the stillness of painting—and perfect silence— his theater would eventually follow. As for Friedrich's painting, and many others like it, Beckett would see through the faddishness of so many movements of painting contemporary to him, and always retain a fresh eye for work that might have been considered passé in other circles. Finding the universal drama throughout all of them, Beckett mined these compositions for his own distinctly visual theater, creating what Whitelaw would refer to as his "paintings."

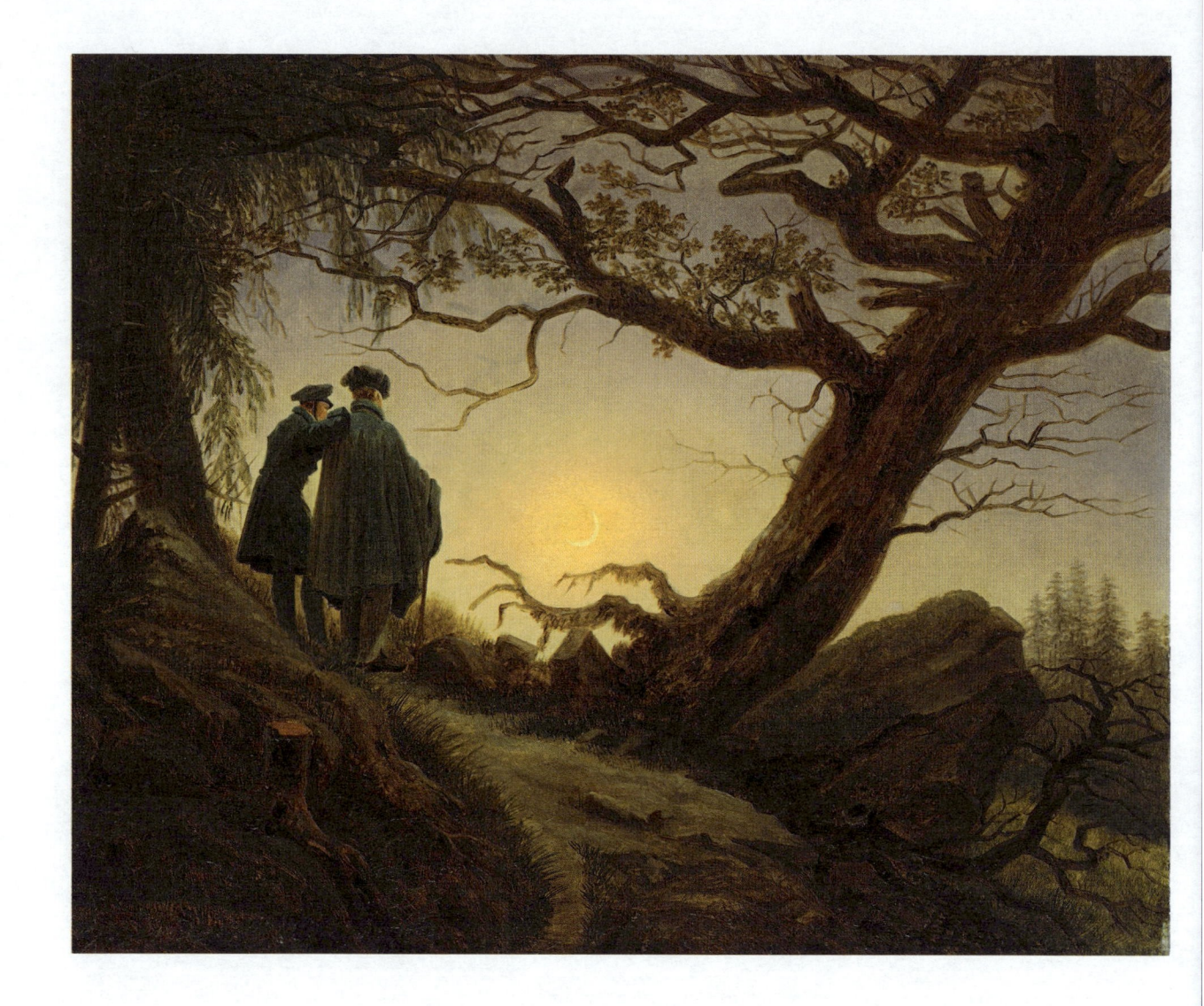

Caspar David Friedrich. *Two Men Contemplating the Moon*, ca. 1830.

atlas

anthony

Legendary Beckett actress Billie Whitelaw once said about Samuel Beckett, "*He writes paintings.*" Aptly put, Whitelaw's comment underscores the visualness of so much of Beckett's work for theater. His plays do appear like paintings —paintings in the historical tradition of the figure, with their stark compositions, dramatic use of lighting, and fragmented evocations of stories. Beckett, it has been shown, actually studied this kind of painting seriously throughout his life, and allowed much of it to inform his dramatic aesthetic.

Whitelaw played roles in a number of Beckett's most visually striking works for theater: *Rockaby*, *Not I*, and *Footfalls*. In all of them, an obvious debt to painting is revealed. Posing like a grieving Mary Magdalene in *Footfalls*, Whitelaw seems closely modeled to the innumerable depictions of the scene conveyed by Renaissance painters. And in *Not I*, in which Whitelaw premiered the lead role, the haunting, floating mouth borrowed candidly from Caravaggio. Indeed, Beckett is on record conceding to this old master's direct influence on *Not I*. Thanks to devoted scholars—friends, actually—of Beckett, such as Ruby Cohn, who recorded Whitelaw's insightful quote above, and Beckett's masterful biographer James Knowlson, it's now known in detail how these references surface in surprising ways in Beckett's work.

As a student at Trinity College in Dublin in the early 1920s, Beckett spent countless hours at the nearby National Gallery of Ireland in Dublin, where he studied the collection's old masters. He was fanatical for its Dutch and Flemish paintings, its van Goyens, El Grecos, and Rembrandts, and especially the *Pietà* by Perugino. Explicit references to the *Pietà* would turn up in Beckett's earliest prose and poetry. At the same time, he also began a lifelong friendship with Thomas MacGreevy, who would later become director of the gallery. In the late 1920s, Beckett failed to professionalize his own passion for painting in a rejected bid to be hired as assistant curator at London's National Gallery.

In 1937, as Germany was mobilizing for war and its escalated campaign against Jews and other minorities, Beckett toured the galleries and museums of Dresden, Munich, and Berlin, and even attended one of the famous Degenerate Art exhibits in Halle. On this very tour, Beckett happened upon the painting that would inspire *Waiting for Godot*: Caspar David Friedrich's *Two Men Contemplating the Moon*. Corroborated in evidence by a directorial notebook for *Waiting for Godot* ("K.D. Friedrich"—Beckett spelled the painter's first name with a "K"—is initialed in a key scene), and admitted personally by Beckett to Ruby Cohn decades after its premiere, it's fascinating how this romantic, 19th-century transcendental painting could ignite the vision of a darkly humorous play that would, as the cliché has it, *change modern theater*.

hishaku

Our kids love sticks. Every time we go to a park they bring home a stick or two. It seems wrong to throw out such carefully chosen objects, so their collection continues to grow. Another unpredictably fun object is the bucket. To a child, a bucket is not simply a means to carry water. It does that, but it can also be a sand-castle maker or a clunky shoe replacement; turned upside down a bucket is a good step stool, helmet, or drum. Simple objects offer countless uses to the playful mind.

While browsing a hardware shop in Tokyo I came across the *hishaku*—a peculiar object that was both a stick and a bucket. I brought it home and immediately the stick-bucket (*hishaku*) became a favorite toy. Not only could it be used to water hard-to-reach plants, but also it successfully helped one brother blast water all over the other. The *hishaku* was then quickly converted into a drum and drumstick in one by banging it on the ground to create a loud cowbell-type sound, loud enough to get the attention of anyone on our street; it was also used as a berry holder, a bath toy, a sword, and a shovel.

Considering the popularity of the *hishaku* with my own children, I began to wonder why I don't see them in more Japanese homes. Surely, it is not the most essential tool in the house and I never hear anyone say, "My *hishaku* is broken! I have to go out and get a new one." (They are actually quite robust.) I guess what keeps most people from rushing out to buy a *hishaku* is that it seems redundant—there are plenty of buckets and cups that could do the same job.

There are animals that, like the *hishaku*, have an unexpected combination of parts. The platypus has the surprising combination of fur and beak in addition to being a mammal that lays eggs. I heard that the platypus, while on land, bends its toes and walks on its knuckles to protect its webbing. Even with these incongruous elements, the platypus exists and this is evidence of its success. Similarly a *hishaku*, lying in the shadows, has a quiet persistence, but its existence is also proof of its success. Both the *hishaku* and the platypus are best adapted to use with water, but they also work well in so many other ways.

I was excited to see a man in Asakusa—the riverside neighborhood where traditional Japanese culture has been preserved—hurriedly scooping boiling-hot water with two *hishakus*, one in each hand. At this moment, it was clear to me that a *hishaku*, or two, could come in handy. It is hard to explain what it is that makes a *hishaku* so satisfying to use. Perhaps it is easier to hold a stick than a cup and being able to reach farther just feels good.

Children are not restrained by names or the intended purpose of things; they are quick to invent new uses for everyday objects. We usually call this "playing" but for children this is a serious endeavor undertaken with complete focus. I've noticed many expensive children's toys that seem to do all the playing while the child passively watches. It is to the credit of children that they tire of these pricey limited toys and move on to much more fascinating objects like cardboard boxes and *hishakus*.

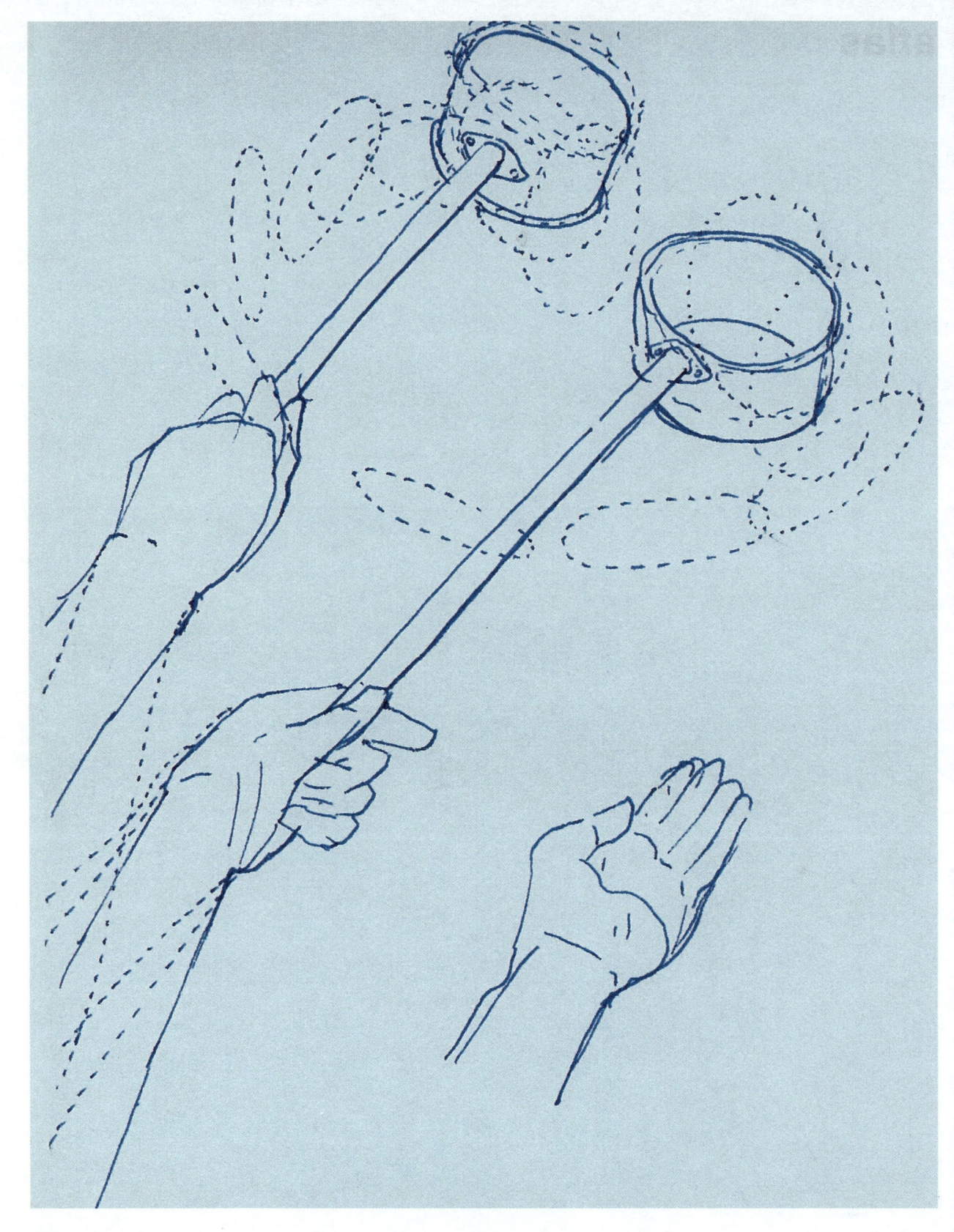

Mike Abelson. *Hishaku Scoop*, 2012.

abelson mike

why eames matters

I have dealt in all things Eames for over twenty-five years and my appreciation for their work continues to grow. Decades after their deaths, I see more and more how much their design work matters.

Eames matters because their designs were functional, problem solving, and rational. More than a chair, an Eames piece suggests a mode of thinking and, by extension, a way of life. Their approach to the design process was marked by rigor and obsessive attention to detail. The furniture still looks right and fresh today because it is.

Eames matters because it is essential. Their design work is everywhere—not only the iconic furniture but the modes of visual communication and design thinking they espoused. The clarity of the design work from the Eames Office is the very seed from which a company like Apple grows. Their design philosophies and sense of self-promotion have been inherited by our contemporary icon of design: Steve Jobs. Think Different. Think Eames.

Eames matters because it is fun. The real magic of the work is the expressive just-so-ness that is always present. Joy is a part of the solution. The emotive qualities of design are not always embraced by modernism, but Eames design has a lightness informed by play. Only Eames could have created the Solar Do-Nothing Machine (1957), a design famous for the beauty by which it achieved its stated goal. Work at the Office was often interrupted for impromptu goofiness, often elaborately documented for the camera. As Charles Eames advised, "Take your pleasures seriously." Their pleasures remain ours to enjoy today.

wright   **richard**

a simple card

Before I was born, my father worked for IBM, as did my uncle. Growing up, my dad always kept the famous THINK sign on his desk—a constant presence every time I visited his office. I remember believing that IBM stood for "International Brotherhood of Magicians." My cousins tried to convince me that it stood for "I've Been Moved," because working as a salesman meant relocating quite a bit. It was not until college that I became conscious of IBM as a design leader. I started out as a fine arts major and switched to graphic design. In 1980, one of my teachers, Tom Coleman, urged me to take a summer course abroad sponsored by Kent State University. It was an opportunity to study design in Switzerland with Paul Rand, the modernist graphic designer responsible for famous identities like IBM, ABC, UPS, Enron, and NeXT. While I did not attend that summer program, I took the opportunity to study with Rand in graduate school at Yale University. As I began to focus more and more on graphic design, specifically corporate identity, I came to see Rand's work for IBM as the gold standard of design with specific and lasting impact.

Later on, I became a collector of design ephemera and began attending paper and antique fairs, where I would always pick up the odd IBM-branded item. When I heard that Rand's library had been sold to the Brattle Book Shop in Boston, I made the trip to see what I could find. I spent most of one morning searching the stacks without much success, until luckily I opened an old book on Mondrian and discovered a page with marginalia that I felt was surely in Rand's handwriting. What made the book even more special was that within its pages I found the business card of Thomas J. Watson Jr.—the president of IBM circa 1956. As corporate titans go, Watson Jr. was certainly one of the most powerful businessmen in America and possibly the world. It was Watson Jr.—the son of IBM founder Thomas Watson—who hired a team of designers to shape the identity of IBM. The team was led by architect and industrial designer Eliot Noyes (a friend of Watson's), who brought on Paul Rand, Charles and Ray Eames, George Nelson, and others to contribute to this effort. Rand was the one to established the guidelines and corporate image of IBM, an ambitious undertaking described vividly in *The Interface: IBM and the Transformation of Corporate Design, 1945–1976* by John Harwood (2011). A version of the original 1956 logo Rand designed for IBM is still in use today.

It was great to find an example of Rand's early work for IBM. The card was designed in Bodoni with the IBM logo blind embossed. Watson's title flush left, in italics, and no phone number. How about that? No flash. No color. Engraved black on off-white stock. Here is one of the most influential executives in the world and his card is simple elegance. I wouldn't have expected anything else.

williams   **jp**

michael cataldi:
tire swings and flower pot holes

Baltimore's official motto is "The Greatest City in America." At least this beats our former slogan, "The City That Reads." Now, before anyone in Wichita or Spokane takes umbrage at this "greatest" claim, let me explain why I've slowly grown to like our motto. Besides the sheer ridiculousness and unverifiability of such a claim, the word "greatest" suggests a certain open-endedness and perhaps even a call to arms. Baltimore is a state of mind, and Baltimore is what you make it.

When I first saw Michael Cataldi's *Tire Swings* and *Flower Pot Hole* series, their elegance, simplicity, and quiet optimism deeply moved me. *Tire Swings* was created during a series of long walks in Baltimore with the artist constructing a tire swing wherever he found a discarded tire. *Flower Pot Hole* is a response to a city ordinance mandating that reported potholes be filled within twenty-four hours, with Cataldi planting flower gardens.

His work is a genuine reminder that I am a human and I live among many others in this city. In the overlooked corners of Baltimore, Cataldi inverts the sadness of a postindustrial America into moments of joy and optimism. As I look at his work, I like to imagine a group of kids laughing as they swing back and forth beneath an aging overpass, or a city work crew perplexed to find a garden planted in the middle of a lonely street.

In some ways these pieces bear for me an emotional similarity to Bruce Springsteen's "Born in the U.S.A.," which also breathes a human fire into the bleakness of a postindustrial nation. Both are elegiac snapshots of urban America that crackle with a new and powerful energy. *Tire Swings* and *Flower Pot Hole* say, "Yes, the past disintegrates, but the present is here for the taking." These spare, poetic gestures convey complex meanings and emotions, reminding me to take a slower look at my surroundings, because this is "The Greatest City in America."

Michael Cataldi. *Flower Pot Hole #1*, 2004.

willen **bruce**

ikko tanaka

Ikko Tanaka is a fantastic Japanese graphic designer whose work I find fascinating. His way of thinking was really interesting and he's most famous for his style that combines traditional Japanese illustrations with a very graphic, colorful, and modern approach. I am particularly fond of a book he released in the 1980s called *Japan Color*. It's over a hundred pages in length but contains nothing but pages filled with blocks of a single color. Amazing!

This book is like a designer's dream. Each page's recto and verso have the same color, but as you flick through the book you realize how different a color can appear in relation to the shade that's sitting on the page opposite it. Put orange next to another hot color and it looks fiery. But put orange next to something more muted and it feels fresh. This makes you realize how powerful color is in determining what you're trying to say.

One of the fabrics I've worked on for Maharam has a pattern called Big Stripe; it's in two rich, dark colorways that I've nicknamed "city colors" and three vibrant colorways that I've called "holiday colors." It's the same pattern in each but the change in shades makes such a difference.

I've always been inspired by color; from the stripes on a beach hut to the gardens at Chelsea Flower Show, you can find inspiration in everything (and if you can't, look again).

smith **paul**

the erstaunliche gugelot car

Collectors of cars can be classified in several categories: the boaster, the investor, the driver, and the Korinthenkacker. The Korinthenkacker are the worst. They are looking for the perfect model, the perfect color, the perfect condition, the perfect provenance. I'm of that latter category . . . as was, most likely, modernist Hans.

Hans Gugelot died in 1965 at the age of forty-five. His professional life was dedicated to the design of industrial products. The SK 55 phonograph, known as the "Schneewittchensarg," the Kodak Diaprojector, and the Braun logo are among his world-famous icons. Gugelot is also thought to be the pioneer of system design and conceived automotive concepts in collaboration with BMW.

The story has it that in 1965 a Gugelot clay model made its way to Porsche: a two-seater with a removable targa roof and retractable headlights. Though Gugelot's model was shunned by Porsche, when the first Porsche 914 rolled out of the factory in 1969, it showed a surprising similarity to Gugelot's design.

Halt die Klappe!

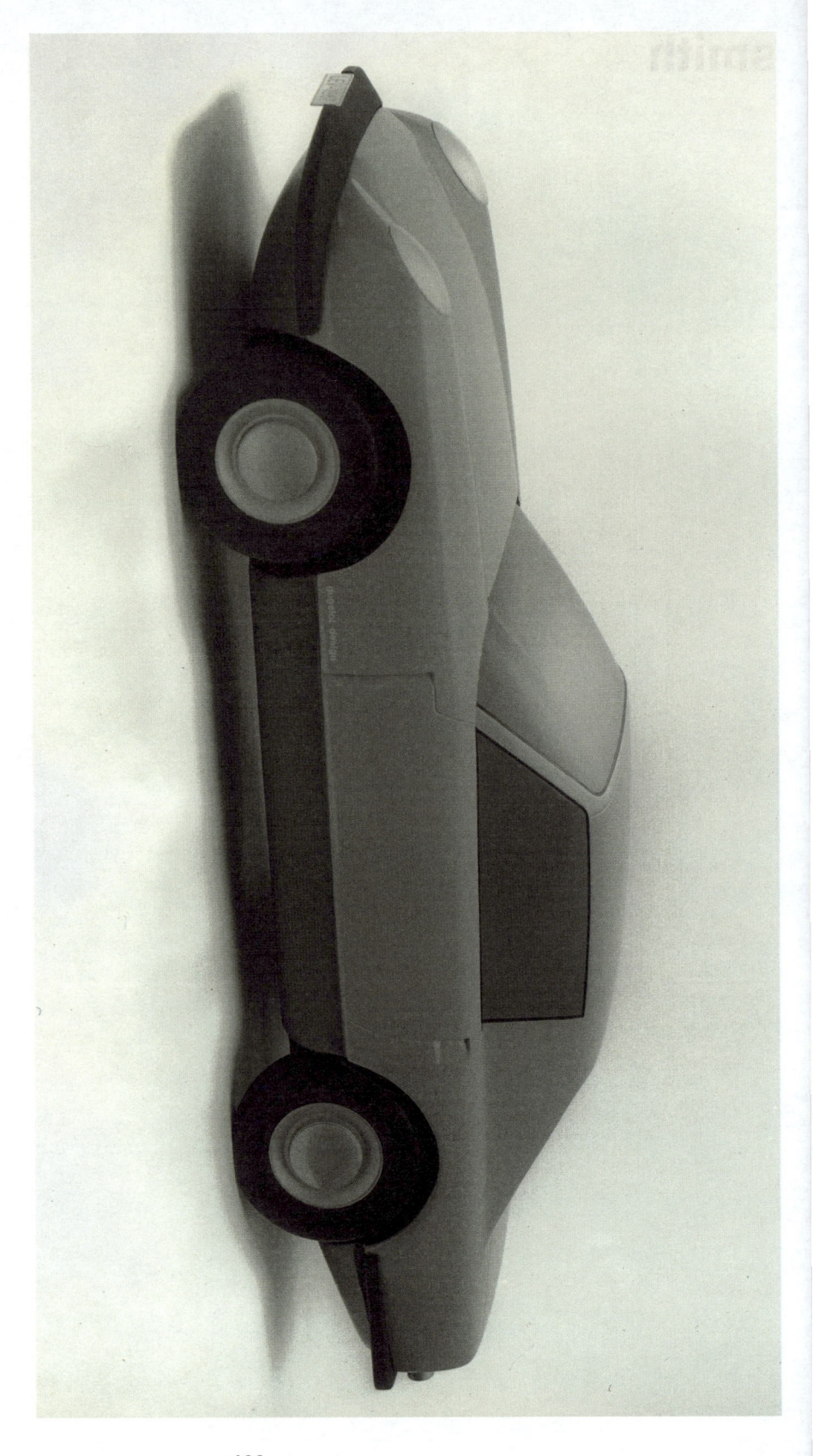

Hans Gugelot. Fastback body for BMW 2000 ti, ca. 1965.

smeets   job

das amazeballs gugelot-auto

Sammler von Autoklassikern lassen sich in unterschiedliche Kategorien unterteilen: der Angeber, der Investor, der Fahrer und der Nit-picker. Am schlimmsten sind die Nit-pickers. Sie suchen das perfekte Modell, die perfekte Farbe, den perfekten Zustand, die perfekte Herkunft. Ich gehöre zu letzterer Kategorie ... und vielleicht Modernist Hans auch.

Hans Gugelot verstarb 1965 im Alter von 45 Jahren. Sein Berufsleben widmete er dem Entwurf industrieller Produkte. The SK55 phonograph 'Snow White's Coffin', der Kodak Diaprojektor „Carousel" und das Braun-Logo sind weltberühmte Ikonen. Gugelot gilt ebenfalls als Wegbereiter des „Systemdesigns" und entwarf in Zusammenarbeit mit BMW Fahrzeugkonzepte.

Der Überlieferung zufolge gelangte ein Gugelot-Ton-Modell 1965 zu Porsche. Ein Zweisitzer mit herausnehmbarem Targa-Dach und Klappscheinwerfern. Diese Version wurde zwar immer entschieden dementiert, aber als der erste Porsche 914 im Jahr 1969 vom Fließband rollte, wies er überraschend viele Ähnlichkeit mit dem vier Jahre jüngeren Entwurf von Gugelot auf.

Shut up!

ben's watch

I contemplated buying a certain fancy watch for years. When I finally gave in and purchased it, I was immediately disappointed by the miniscule amount of enjoyment this expensive item provided.

My client Ben Cohen, the co-founder of the ice cream company Ben & Jerry's, wears a cheap plastic watch I designed for him that features a dial design showing how the U.S. government spends over half of its budget on the Pentagon.

But Ben did not just order one single watch, he bought five thousand and gives one to (almost) everyone he encounters. Both of our interns received one within five minutes of meeting him and wear them proudly—I'm sure they tell their friends how the Ben of Ben & Jerry's had given them their watch.

Ben's cheap watch tells the time just as well as my expensive one does, but it generates much more joy for him and those around him. I am ashamed to admit that his five thousand watches came in at the same price as my single one. Ben's purchase works for him, while I am paying for mine. But then, he is Ben and I am not.

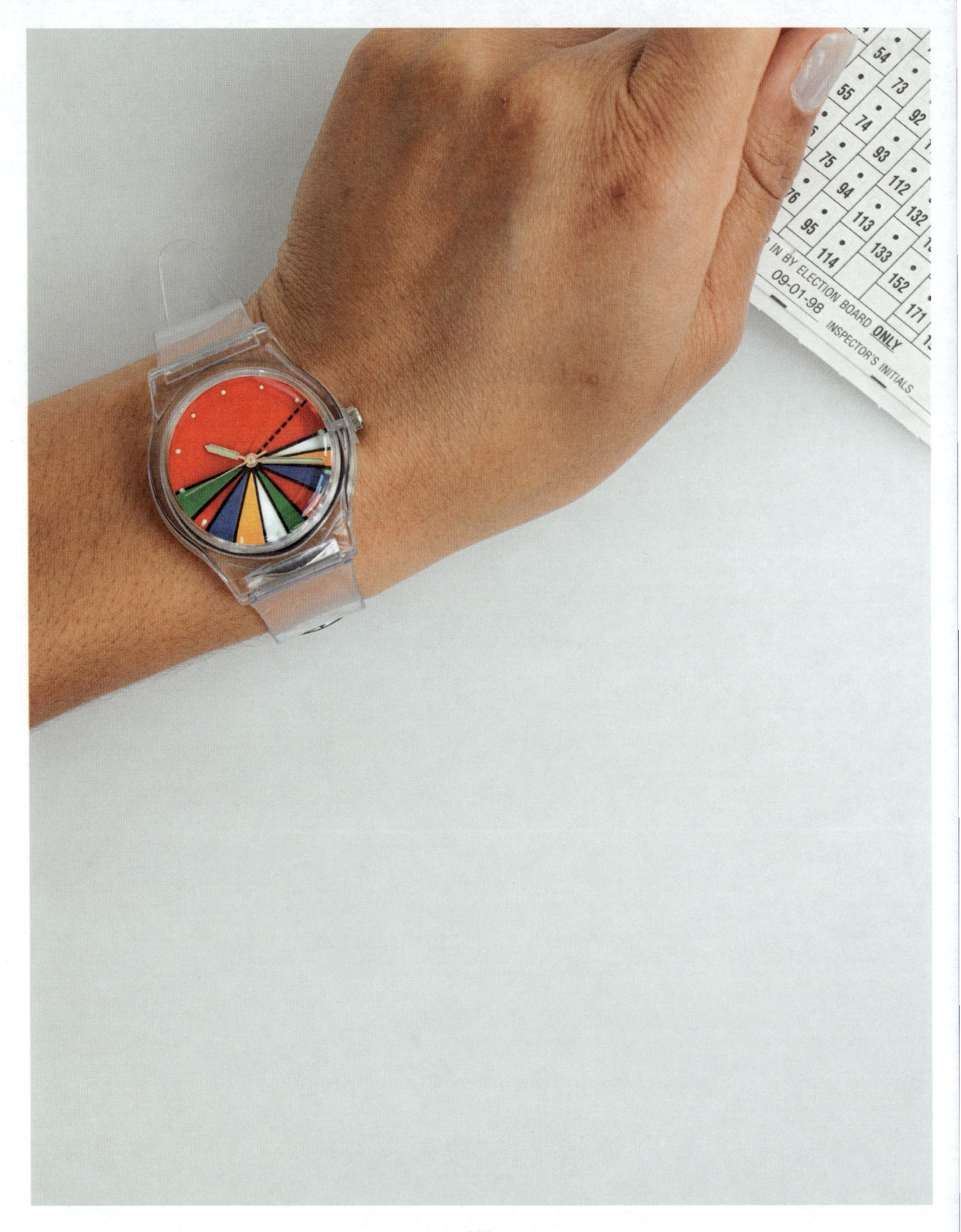

sagmeister **stefan**

the school of constructed realities

Today we visited a new school of design developed specifically to meet the challenges and conditions of the 21st century. It offers only one degree, an MA in Constructed Realities. Having sat through the presentations for the open day, we were still a little unclear about its distinctions between real realities, unreal realities, real unrealities, and unreal unrealities, but we were intrigued enough to want to know more.

The school provides a mix of theory, practice, and reflection. There are no disciplines in the conventional sense; instead, students study bundles of subjects. Some that caught our attention were "Rhetoric, Ethics, and Critical Theory" combined with "Impossible Architecture"; "Scenario Making and Worldbuilding" mixed with "Ideology and Found Realities"; and "CGI and Simulation Techniques" taught alongside "The History of Propaganda, Conspiracy Theories, Hoaxes, and Advertising." Projects are expressed through various forms of reality: mixed, immersive, simulated, unmediated, and so on. Students can also attend the classes "Multiverses and Branding," "The Suspension, Destruction, and Production of Disbelief," "Reality Fabrication: Bottom Up or Top Down?," "The Politics of the Unreal," "Reality: Local Variations," and our favorite, "The Aesthetics of Unreality."

After the presentations we asked the director about the thinking behind the school. He was a little reticent at first, which is understandable knowing the risks associated with relocating design from its cozy home in the old reality-based community to a new one among reality makers, fabricators, and constructors, but he was keen to share. He began by explaining that in his view, for most people today reality isn't working, that it broke sometime near the end of the 20th century:

"It's clear that reality only works for a privileged minority, but designers advocate a realist approach, which means they work within the constraints of reality as it is, for the minority. The school aims to challenge this by making reality a little bit bigger to provide more room for different kinds of dreams and hopes. An important part of this process is generating multiple versions of reality, and this is where design comes in."

"We concluded," he said, "that the only way to challenge this unsatisfactory situation was to be unrealistic—to breach realism's heavily policed borders and to fully embrace unreality."

Listening to him, we began to think so too.

Filip Dujardin. *Untitled*, from the series Fiction, 2007.

dunne and raby

anthony and fiona

a man not meant to stand

Tennessee Williams had a gift for transforming the world around him that extended far beyond Broadway. His lifestyle—which oscillated between bohemianism and celebrity—kept him in constant circuitous travel between New York, Provincetown, St. Louis, New Orleans, and Key West. He had, by way of the particular force of his personality—a combination of dandyish self-assertion, acute humanity, and rampant sexual imagination—the ability to mark these deeply storied locations with extra glamour and gravitas. His suave, sophisticated, and sensual itinerary transcended ordinary travel and gave mid-century America, at least in the minds of the intelligentsia, a more nuanced and subtle character.

In snapshots and publicity photographs Williams is nearly invariably seated. This collection of chairs represents something liminal yet "at-home," a repository for his colloquial and patrician postures, which when taken together tell a story of a transnational jet-setting avant-garde. Beginning with the sober self-discipline of a Spartan wooden chair faced with a typewriter as a young man in St. Louis (and there is no more elemental theater prop than the stark wooden chair); to the solid Arts and Crafts chair, the Victorian interior gloom of New Orleans, and the volatile ether from which he would fashion *A Streetcar Named Desire* (a success against which all subsequent efforts would be measured); to the ubiquitous satin armchairs of luxury hotel lobbies and suites, soft markers for the itinerant and the escapist; and finally the rattan iterations in southern Florida in which he would seek stillness—chairs like little slatted rafts around which heaved the dark tide of success. Ensconcing oneself in a chair, for most a passive action, allowed his personality to activate a place.

In the 1960s Williams had a predilection for falling flat on his face, playing dead (or, indeed, dying for an instant), which he routinely employed as an exit strategy for any conversation or party too taxing for his constitution. This is not to be mistaken for a lack of stamina, for no excesses of the night before would ever encumber his next morning's work, but the effects of pills and drink, his constant companions, did make a hazard out of being upright. The less comfortable state of standing erect was, for Williams, a diminished position for occupation, presence, observation, and other precious forms of sensory intake needed for his being's primary impulse: to write. With Southern grace his speech and body were unhurried, always nestled, lumbar and loin, on a hard or cushioned chair, in an attitude of reception. If psychogeography describes the effects of place on the emotions, then what Williams could manifest was the inverse: his emblematic chair, much like a prie-dieu adding some comfort to devotion, was a quotidian object of mystical purpose.

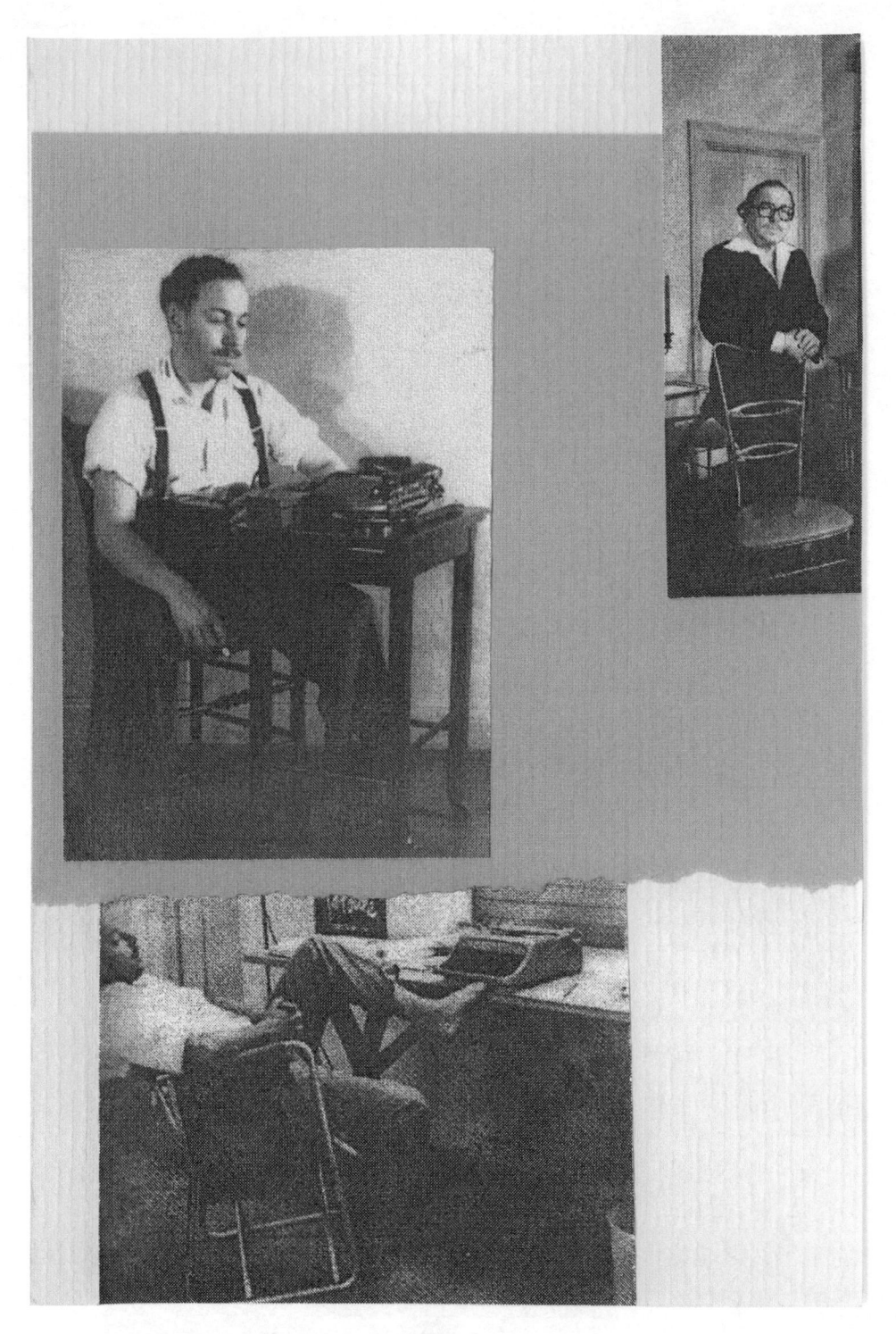

Paul P. *Untitled (Tennessee Williams)*, 2014.

p. **paul**

cortex cast

The euphoria about digital manufacturing ended abruptly when the design template for the Liberator, a 3-D printed handgun, was posted online by Defense Distributed, a group of American design provocateurs who were making a political statement about what they regard as the futility of gun control legislation in the United States. Coincidentally, they also illustrated the terrifying implications of failing to ensure that the development of such powerful technologies is intelligently designed to prevent them from being hijacked for sinister ends, including the covert manufacture of unlicensed weapons.

By alerting us to such perils, the Liberator made a compelling case for the importance of thoughtful and sensitive design, but a design project that sets out to improve people's lives, as the Cortex Cast does, can do so more eloquently.

Jake Evill made his prototype cast from seventeen ounces of nylon plastic using the 3-D scanner from an Xbox Kinect game system and a 3-D printer. He hopes that eventually people's broken limbs can be scanned while they are being treated in a hospital, then their bespoke casts can be manufactured on conveniently located 3-D printers. There is much to be resolved before that happens, but Evill has already created a beautiful piece of design.

Some design projects are deemed beautiful because they are visually seductive. Others are blessed with sensual allure or evocative histories. Yet there are also design endeavors that, like the Cortex Cast, owe their beauty to their designers' intentions.

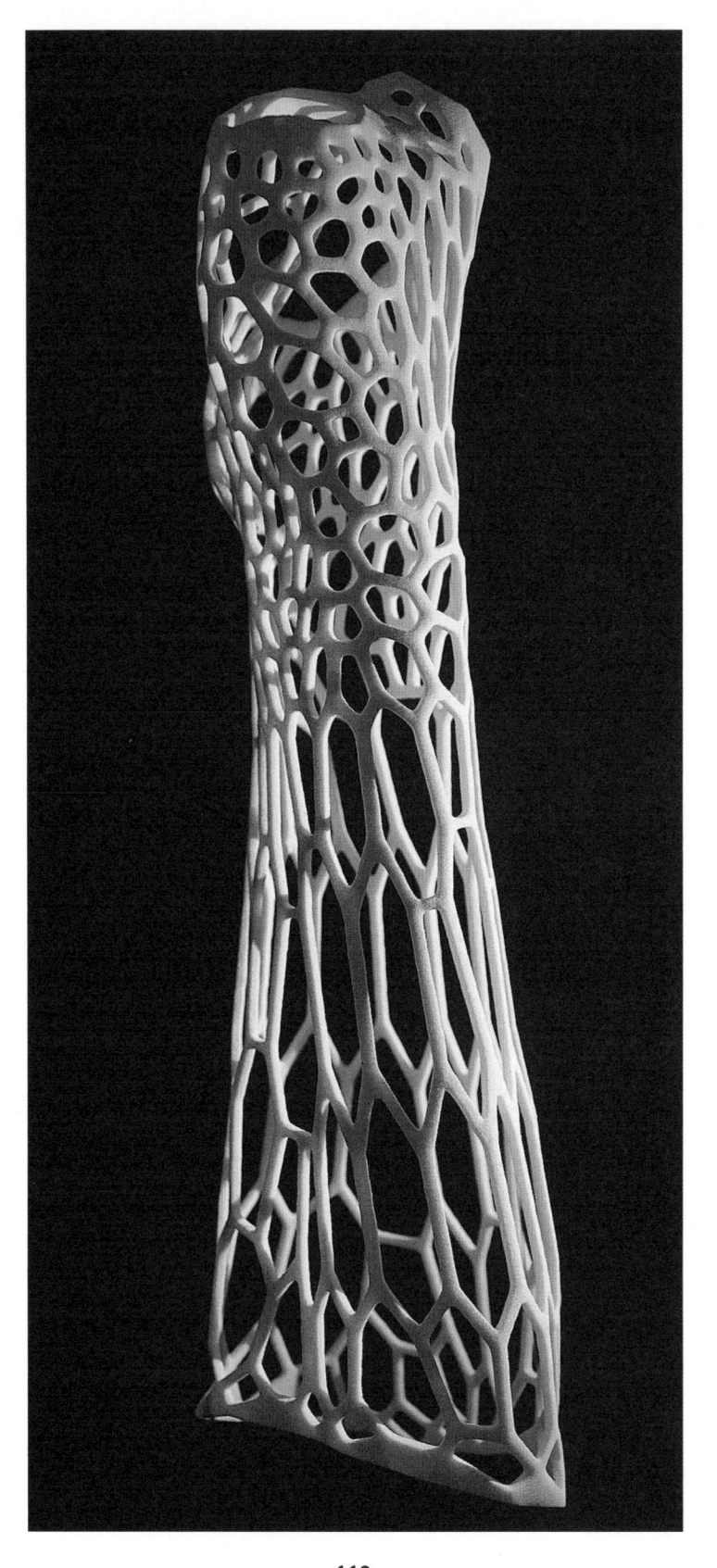

rawsthorn alice

Not so long ago, if you had visited a student design show, many of the wannabe designers would have seemed hellbent on becoming as rich and famous as Philippe Starck—hopefully more so.

These days, young designers are more likely to want to purge poverty, save the biosphere, or do something else to change the world for the better than outswagger Starck. Not all of the new design altruists will succeed, but some might, and even those that don't will have the consolation of having failed in good causes.

One of my favorite examples of a benevolent design-in-progress is the Cortex Cast. The intent behind it is to use 3-D printing to produce bespoke casts for broken limbs that will not only be lighter, cleaner, and more comfortable than traditional plaster ones, but also help the healing process by providing support for the limb where it is needed the most.

It is the work of Jake Evill, who hit upon the idea of designing a customizable cast as his graduation project from Victoria University in Wellington, New Zealand, after breaking his hand in a fight. (This isn't quite as brutal as it sounds: he entered the fray to help a friend.) Hauling around a couple of pounds of dirty, smelly, itchy plaster for several months prompted him to consider whether it would be possible to deploy 3-D printing or another of the new digital production technologies to save other people from the suffering he had undergone.

Devising useful applications for new technologies has been one of design's most important functions throughout history. As complex and elusive as design has been in its multifarious guises, it has always had one unwavering role as an agent of change, one that interprets new developments in other spheres in the hope of ensuring that they will affect us positively, rather than negatively.

Evill is not the only young designer to have been dazzled by the possibilities of digital manufacturing systems, like 3-D printing, which is so fast and precise that it can make objects individually, thereby enabling them to be customized. The first affordable 3-D printers have churned out an awful lot of decorative knick-knacks but some useful things too. As the technology evolves, it promises not only to transform the design process by enabling the people who will use the end product to personalize it, but also offer environmental benefits by wasting less material during production and better repair breakages by making accurate replicas of damaged components.

etel adnan

Over the course of the 1960s, Adnan started to move away from the purely abstract forms. In 1964, thanks to a fellow artist in San Francisco, she discovered *leporellos*, accordion-style folded books in which she could mix drawing with writing and poetry. Another pivotal moment took place a decade later, when Adnan moved to Sausalito, near San Francisco, and discovered the landscape of Mount Tamalpais, which remains the most important encounter of her life. Her obsession with the mountain led to many paintings and, after more than two decades of intense contemplation, to the seminal book *Journey to Mount Tamalpais* (1986), which explores links between nature and art. As Adnan told me, "Mount Tamalpais became my house. For Cézanne, Sainte-Victoire was no longer a mountain. It was an absolute. It was painting." Mount Tamalpais also appears in another dimension of Adnan's work, her seventy filmic snapshots of the sea, sun, and sky, which she started to make in the 1980s with a Super 8 camera. On visits to New York City, she would also film what she saw from her window. The bridges, skylines, and passing ships that she observed there lead us to yet another dimension in her practice: her drawings and watercolors, which she has made daily ever since she began to draw as her means of expression while learning English in America. These New York drawings, made with thick black ink, were soon after followed by a series of drawings of the stone bridges of Paris. As Simone Fattal shows in her writings on Adnan's visual art practice, one of these is an echo of a line in a Baudelaire poem, "an agonizing sun falling under an arch."

It was in Paris that I met Adnan for the first time, in 2007. We quickly became friends and started to collaborate on many projects, such as the Serpentine Gallery's Edgware Road Project and several marathons between London and Athens and the *Point d'Ironie* magazine with agnès b. We began to record a large number of conversations. Adnan is one of the greatest artists of our time, one of the wisest I have ever met, and a great inspiration to many people. Although she is now in her late eighties, I am always struck by the amazing energy and intensity of her recent practice, which is still among the best work being created in the world today. I am also continually struck by the amazing optimism of her paintings, which as Fattal explains, both "exude energy and give energy. They grow on you like talismans . . . paintings as pure energy with which to live one's life with courage."

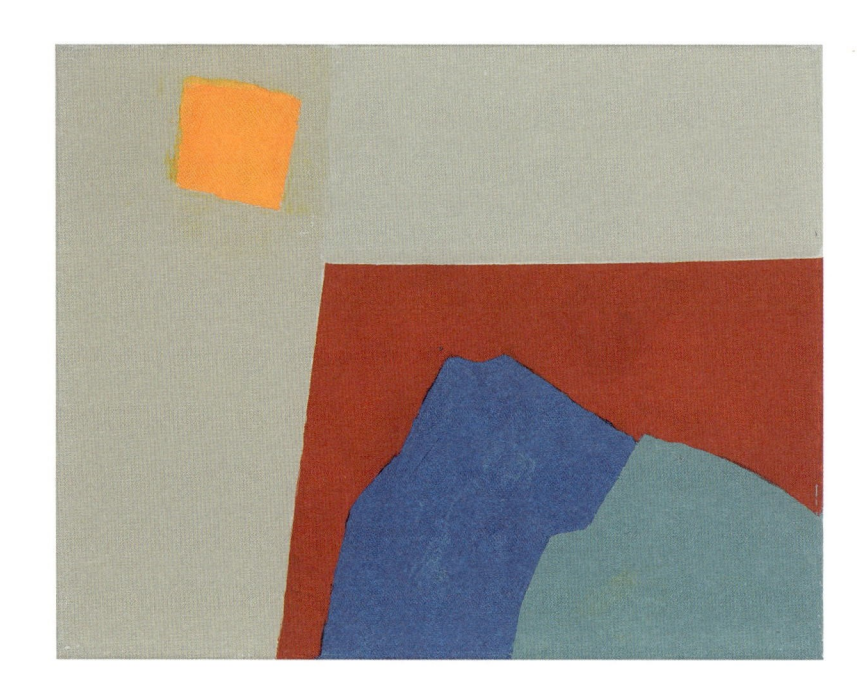

Etel Adnan. *Untitled (204)*, 2013.
Etel Adnan. *Untitled (200)*, 2013.

obrist hans ulrich

"Decent or beautiful public work is democratic, because even a poor person can walk in a beautiful environment and have his spirit uplifted. We painters do an elitist type of work; nevertheless it has its place because it's intellectual and spiritual. But we badly need public works."

Dear Michael,

I hope you are very well. This is a cyber-introduction. When we met last month in London, our conversation about William Morris, Arts and Crafts, and, to quote Gilbert and George, "ART FOR ALL," made me suddenly think that it is very urgent you meet Etel Adnan. Etel's work has many dimensions and, like William Morris, her *Gesamtkunstwerk* includes poetry, novels, translations, activism, art, drawings, notebooks, and also textile and carpet designs. Adnan has a strong conviction that we have to go beyond the gallery and reinvent public art—her belief in "art for everyone" links her to Morris.

The very first work I saw by Etel Adnan was a long Japanese folding book in which handwritten poems and signs were combined with drawings. I was immediately and magnetically attracted by its energy; I wanted to know more. The next day, I started to read *Sitt Marie Rose* (1977), her masterpiece and the great novel of the Lebanese civil war. The day after that, I read her extraordinary *The Arab Apocalypse* (1989), which addresses the turmoil of war in the Arabic world beyond Lebanon and made Adnan one of the world's most important political writers, as well as a key protagonist of the peace movement. I then ordered dozens of other books by Adnan, and became increasingly aware of the many dimensions of her writing: reportage, fiction, plays, and her outstanding recent poetry collections such as *Sea and Fog* (2012) and *Seasons* (2008), in which natural and meteorological phenomena are presented as nontangible things that imperceptibly influence and transform our skins and our souls. This was the first time since high school—when I read every single word that Robert Walser had ever written, including his "micrograms"—that I had felt the urgent need to read the complete works of a writer.

Reading Adnan is addictive. As the legendary Palestinian poet Mahmoud Darwish once said, she has never written a bad line. Etel Adnan was born in 1925 in Beirut. In the late 1950s, after her studies at the Sorbonne and at Harvard, she taught philosophy at the University of California and started to paint. Her earliest works were abstract compositions with squares of colors directly applied from the tube. Often a red square was the pivotal point of the composition. As Adnan told me, she was interested in the immediate beauty of color. During her initial years in California, she also started to make her first colorful abstract tapestries. These works, influenced by an interest in oriental rugs, are a separate dimension of her practice that she has pursued ever since. Never translating her existing paintings into tapestries, she uses specific designs for her textile works, through which she celebrates the vibrancy of the wool.

movement

This is a photograph of an installation in Chicago titled *Striated Presentation Striated*. It shows two people preparing cloth to hang on my display structure. I took the photo when I went to check the installation of the work the day before the trade showroom opened to clients. There is a deep history that connects exhibition display to commercial display. In the 1950s, artist Richard Hamilton made use of this complex set of cross-references to create work that was—in its most extreme form—pure display. Yet it is not the structure I want to talk about here. It is the action I caught in motion while struggling with limited light that morning in Chicago. For here can be found the evocative moment for me. It is the human body moving with fabric.

I am old enough to have had homemade clothes. I would go with my mother when she bought cloth to make things for me, such as denim for homemade jeans that made other mothers sigh with sympathy at my no-brand plight and my bravery. I fought her over these homemade garments. But I never confessed to her how much I was entranced by the process itself of buying the cloth. Watching the man (it was always a man) pulling down a roll of fabric and swiftly pulling it out across a flat table that carried a measuring mark along one edge. Pulling, bunching, and pulling again—swiftly reaching the required length and adding a little more before speeding scissors across the weave. The sense of stock as a length or roll to be stored for years or sold out within days seemed abstract and full of potential. I saw something of that man's facility with material that morning in Chicago. Something fundamental and toward something more.

gillick **liam**

accidents will happen

Few things in life ever come out as you planned them. My daughter's father is a photographer. But when he disappeared from the picture, I became our resident documentarian by default.

My declaration of independence was to buy a camera. I didn't want anything fancy or expensive. Just a no-frills point-and-shoot. Without much persuasion, the young man at my local shop steered me to a Holga, the idea being that if you are going to buy a cheap camera, you might as well buy a cheap camera.

First introduced in China in 1981, the Holga was designed as an accessible, medium-format camera for the Chinese working class to document important family events. (A 35mm version would come later.) Costing around forty dollars, a Holga is certainly not a "good" camera. Some go so far as to call it a crappy camera. It is often referred to as a toy camera. Its features are few, the shutter speed is fixed, and pretty much every component is made of plastic, including the lens.

Photos taken with a Holga often come out blurry or distorted or disfigured by light flares. Sometimes they come out blank. But Holga devotees stand by this camera, because of and not in spite of its defects. It is often used in schools as a teaching tool—mistakes: learn from them, embrace them. This was exactly what I needed to hear.

"You will miss a lot of special moments," a friend who makes her living as a photographer warned me. These words rang in my head as I looked through the first batch of prints. Light flares blotted out my daughter's face. A couple of photos were double exposed where I forgot to advance the film. Most of the photos could not even be generously described as "experimental."

A few of them are beautiful. Ultimately, they are a testament to the fact that my daughter's childhood is inevitably going to be an imperfect one—and also to the fact that I am there to witness it, flares and all.

browne

alix

a rose is a rose is a rose is

When I was working with Hella Jongerius on the presentation at Moss of her textile design, Repeat, she explained to me her beautiful intent of repeating the many patterns woven into this complex textile by applying them to other media, specifically porcelain bowls and vases and plates. A leap was made across materials and functions and production methods: all categories of objects were treated as suitable surfaces for identical decoration.

This reminded me of something.

In 1959 my parents built their dream house in a suburb of Chicago; Robert M., a young man who had become the "family decorator," was to work with us again. His word was law.

Bob M.'s particular forte (and in my young opinion, his saving grace) was his extreme application of pattern. He would select a fabric—say, an 18th-century French toile, rose color on a cream ground—and apply this fabric to *all* surfaces and to *all* objects in the room. The silhouettes of the individual furnishings nearly vanished in this sea of identical pattern, like summer-stock scenery where the painted backdrops have built-in doors so that suddenly the "ocean" opens and a stagehand walks in.

Where the textile could not be applied—for example, the wooden floor moldings or the cabinet hardware—Mr. M. would have "fine painters" reproduce the pattern in oils, so that each object would be fully patterned. Even the sink in the bedroom, my father's dream extravagance, was enameled with the French pattern.

This man was not kidding around.

The result was something surreal: I would watch my mother fold herself into the wallpaper as she climbed into bed; I would see my father float on air as his chair disappeared into the walls and surrounding furniture; and when I slowly drew open the Venetian blinds covered in that same textile, it was as if a kind of surgery was being performed on the room—a skinning of sorts.

I loved that house, and I wonder if people still do that today. . . .

Sandy Skoglund. *The Cocktail Party*, 1992.

moss **murray**

vivianna torun bülow-hübe

Her pieces are unmistakable. Outspoken works of sinuous sensuality, her collars and pendants follow the anatomy, nestling in the hollow at the base of the throat, or dangling down the back so they move while dancing. They are intended to accentuate the human body's natural beauty. For Torun, jewelry was about the basic human need for ritual embellishment. "I dream of making jewelry that is so near to being feminine that you wear it all the time, you live with it on"—pieces to be worn for hanging out the washing as well as for special occasions. Her works were always *pour etre, pas pour paraitre* ("for being, not appearing to be"). Timelessness was at the core of her philosophy. She believed that people should "have things that touch their hearts, and have them for decades. In our disposable, materialistic times we have none of the content left, none of the essence of life. Adornment has lost its true innocence."

She wasn't interested in precious stones, preferring simple things like pebbles, granite, moonstone, and rock crystal. In an artistic parallel world to Ursula Andress meeting 007 while hunting for shells in *Dr. No*, Torun met Picasso while hunting for pebbles on the beach.

She never stopped working. "I always needed to eat. Bills needed to be paid. But I need to work too. There are still masses of ideas I want to formulate. I'm no good with words—I'd rather speak through the silver." Although the majority of her work was in jewelry, she also turned her hand to other areas including sculpture, cutlery, and china, applying her appreciation of the human form to her other pieces. "It's about how it feels in the hand, how it fits in the mouth. About tiny, everyday detail."

crawford

ilse

Fate deals some strange cards. It is curious that perhaps the most well-known piece by legendary silversmith Vivianna Torun Bülow-Hübe (better known as Torun) is a wristwatch. In 1962 when she was asked to design an object of dislike for an exhibition called *Antagonism II* at the Musée des Arts Décoratifs alongside Picasso et al, she decided to do a watch with no hour hand or numbers because she said, she "abhorred the relentlessness of time." There was only a second hand and a mirrored back, to remind the wearer of the moment. To remind that life is now. Five years later, with her third marriage behind her and children, grandchildren, dogs, cats, and kittens to support, to her great relief Georg Jensen stepped in and put the watch into production, adding the requisite hour and minute hands and putting bread on the table.

The daughter of a town planner and a sculptress, she was one of the first female silversmiths to achieve renown. She set up her workshop in the late 1940s, and throughout her life produced work that led the way for modern jewelry.

It could very easily have gone another way. At the end of the World War II she left her native Malmö on a sailboat for a party in Denmark and came home pregnant. But she persisted in her ambition to go to college to train as a silversmith. She paid her way by selling her pieces as she went along. When she couldn't afford raw materials she worked in rattan and brass wire, creating a fashion for collars in the African style. Two marriages and two children later she found herself in Paris, where she met her third husband, the African American painter Walter Coleman. With him she lived at the hub of the Paris jazz scene, hanging out with Charlie Mingus, Bud Powell, and Billie Holiday, for whom she made many of her avant-garde pieces. And she was active in the Black Is Beautiful movement. However in those days Paris was not kind to mixed couples so they headed south, now with two more children in tow, to the Riviera, where they rented a place in Biot ("the place was swarming with life"). Later she went to Germany to be near a Subud community, and then to Jakarta, where she worked with a charitable organization teaching local teenagers to make jewelry. "You know if ten people have work, a hundred will be able to eat."

While her life was an extraordinary helter-skelter, her vision for silver was clear from the outset. When I interviewed her back in 1995, she talked about how from the very beginning she was at odds with her times, with the dressy, showy school of jewelry, with the idea of jewelry as status. She worked with silver because it was a material "from which I can coax a fluid, curving movement." She was fascinated by the vortex, "this movement which penetrates all of the universe, from the galaxies to the smallest molecule of DNA. Everything around us swirls—the vortex symbolizes to me the vibrations of life, infinity, heavenly creation." As a girl her passion was for ice-skating, and in many ways her relationship with silver reflected the one she had with the ice. "When I work with silver I perceive within my whole being the curves, the turns, like when my skates were tracing precise and slow figures on the ice. . . . It took a lot of discipline and physical awareness to make those fine curves, a continual balancing of the inner and outer edges of the blades."

altmann & kühne

How Loos must have hated Altmann & Kühne. Hoffmann conceived it as a fairy-tale candy store with exquisitely made chocolates perching neatly on paper doilies amid the gleaming wood, brass, and glass of the cabinets and shelves crafted at the Wiener Werkstätte. The packaging hailed from there too: dozens of boxes in different shapes and sizes, emblazoned with vividly colored castles, flowers, waltzing couples, toy soldiers, dogs, horses, candy stalls (no prizes for guessing whose), and fairground rides that could have come from the pages of beautifully illustrated children's books.

The same images were printed in muted gold on the creamy white paper bags in which the chocolates were wrapped, and blown up as cameos on the walls. A Viennese chocolate lover walking into Altmann & Kühne in the 1930s would have been taken back to the city's imperial glory as the capital of a global super-power before the collapse of the Austro-Hungarian Empire after World War I.

Sadly, the Wiener Werkstätte closed in 1932 following years of financial struggle, but the picturesque chocolate store, so lovingly crafted by its artisans, flourished. When Austria was annexed by Nazi Germany in 1938, Mr. Altmann and Mr. Kühne, both Jewish, fled to the United States. They entrusted the Graben store to loyal employees, who continued to run it as their absent bosses had done, just as their successors do today.

No matter how busy I am on visits to Vienna, I always find time to check in on Hoffmann's *Gesamtkunstwerk* at Altmann & Kühne. The façade is a little faded, but the wood, brass, and glass is polished meticulously, and the boxes and bags look as playful as they must have done when the originals were rolling off the Wiener Werkstätte's printing presses. The chocolates taste as delicious as ever, and there is not a palm tree to be seen, artificial or otherwise.

rawsthorn alice

One of the dreams shared by the architects, artists, and craftsmen who belonged to the Wiener Werkstätte craft workshops in early 20th-century Vienna was to produce a *Gesamtkunstwerk*, which translates loosely from German as a "complete work of art," or one that includes lots of different art forms. From time to time, they succeeded, and among my favorites is the Altmann & Kühne chocolate store that opened on the Graben in the heart of Vienna during the early 1930s.

It was designed by Josef Hoffmann, one of the most influential Austrian architects of the time, who had co-founded the Werkstätte in 1903 with the sculptor Koloman Moser. A draconian character, Hoffmann only ever dressed in black, gray, or white, adhered to the same strict daily schedule, and was so persnickety about other people that he would disappear into a private room (specially reserved for the purpose) whenever anyone he disliked threatened to enter his office. Predictably, he frequented a few carefully chosen restaurants and coffee houses, once fleeing from a regular haunt, never to return, after spotting an artificial palm tree there.

Equally fastidious in his choice of clients, Hoffmann had worked for Emile Altmann and Ernst Kühne before, having designed their first store in 1928. Their chocolates, which were made by hand to their own recipes, became so sought after in Vienna that they decided to open a second store on the Graben, and commissioned Hoffmann to design the façade and interior, including all of its contents, even the bags and boxes.

The result is typical of Hoffmann's work in that period, being inspired both by the geometric simplicity of the architecture of Le Corbusier, Walter Gropius, and other modern movement pioneers and by the ornate aesthetic of Vienna's craft heritage. The exterior owed more to modernism, being divided between a wide window and a white screen bearing the owners' names, but inside Hoffmann indulged the love of fantasy and folklore for which he was regularly lambasted by more ascetic contemporaries, notably his arch rival, Adolf Loos.

whistler's rooms

For an artist with no prominent disciples, James Abbott McNeill Whistler has left a curious and broadly applied aesthetic legacy. He was an extreme dandy as well as obstinate reformer, never without a battle being waged in the papers or courtroom. Paradoxically, his fame now rests mostly on a maudlin appreciation of "Whistler's Mother," a painting whose real title is *Arrangement in Grey and Black, No. 1* (1871). Whistler often titled his works with such terms as "Arrangements," "Harmonies," and "Notes," placing their compositional structures beyond the sentimental mores of Victorian art to evoke the abstraction of music. Whistler was among the first Western artists to embrace the art of Japan, eventually subsuming its comparatively radical dimensionality into his practice.

Whistler's aesthetics extended to the rooms themselves in which his art was presented. Anticipating the gallery as we know it today, these radical spaces can be considered among the first iterations of installation art. The dark, fabric-covered walls of the time were replaced with painted neutral surfaces; art was disentangled from the 19th-century practice of dense, salon-style clusters and placed on an even line; brass nameplates were replaced with the gallery checklist; lighting was regulated and controlled through ceiling-mounted blinds over skylights. Furniture, flowers, and floor coverings were all part of a complex design within a unified color scheme that came to define the exhibitions, such as *Arrangement in White and Yellow* (1884), where every detail was part of a harmonious orchestration, down to the livery of the gallery attendant. The effect was certainly controversial for Whistler's period, when the intensity of such color palettes were thought to induce sickness.

Whistler was deeply in love with his effects and found sport in humiliating those who weren't. A certain queerness can be ascribed to Whistler—fey and petite, an American in London, beauty was his religion. Oscar Wilde, a friend and verbal sparring mate, was most in debt for his own highly developed aesthetic to Whistler. It was famously after one of Whistler's high-profile provocations that Wilde said, "I wish I'd said that," to which Whistler retorted, "You will, Oscar, you will."

Although there are no extant examples save for the Peacock Room (1876–77) —a masterpiece of intervention, if not vandalism, on the artist's part—one of Whistler's greatest achievements was within domestic interior design. In his own home he was at his most radical: sparse, light-filled rooms with clean, painted walls of white and yellow; Japanese fans and blue-and-white china purposefully placed; slender, uncomfortable cane chairs, positioned as carefully as the decorative objects; and a few of his own etchings, simply framed. Whistler held aristocratic pretensions in art, but his domestic rooms were pure and economical. Fortune saw him alternately rich and ruined, yet, with each change of circumstance between London and Paris, he found opportunities for refinement. In later years, his white-painted environments contained but a few perfectly placed trunks and boxes —a sense of space so mutant from its overstuffed time period as to forecast the art gallery of the future, and, by extension, contemporary interior design.

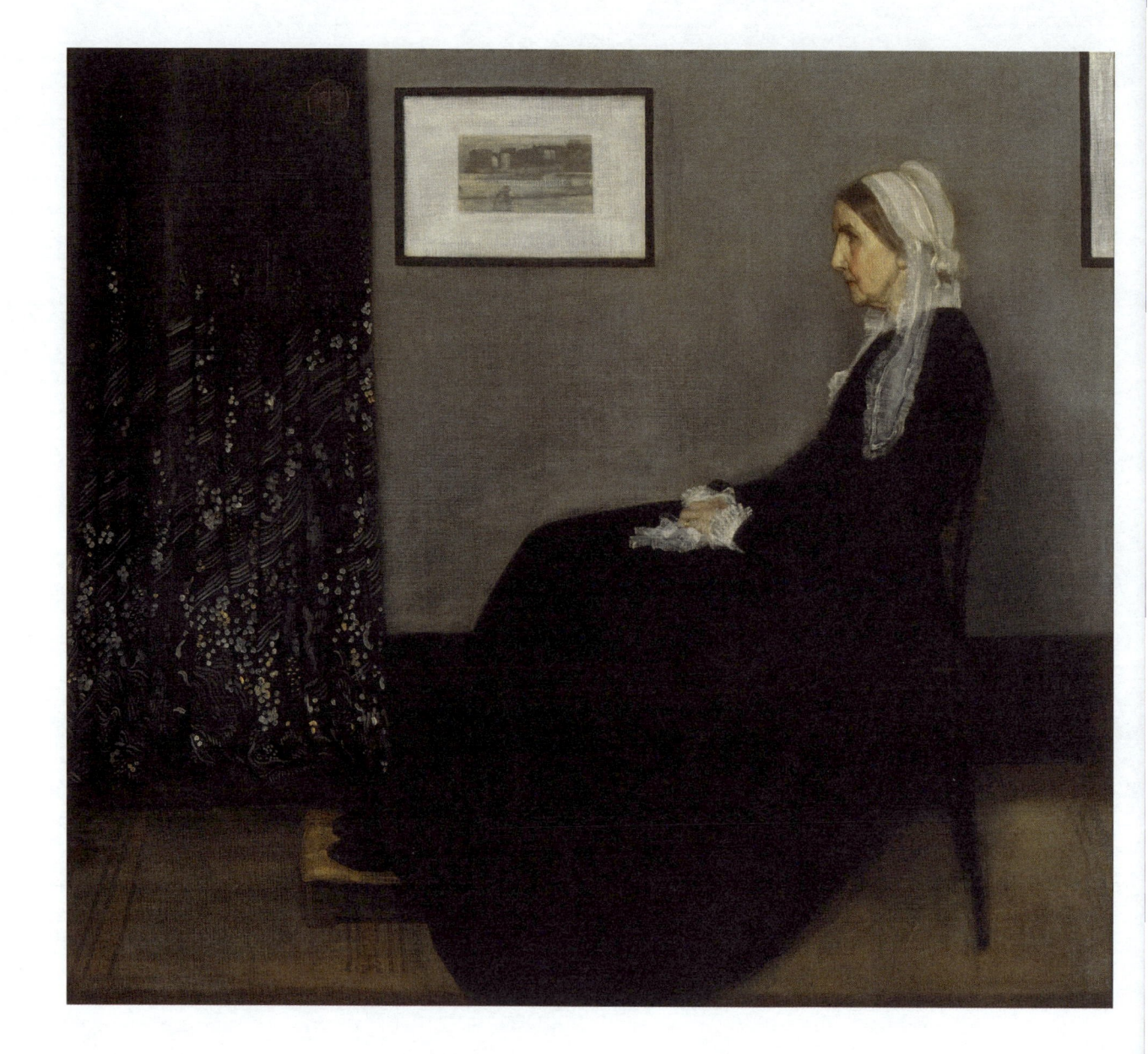

James Abbott McNeill Whistler.
Arrangement in Grey and Black, No. 1, 1871.

p. paul

the sweater baron of key west

In the southernmost city of the lower forty-eights, it's always sweater season for someone somewhere else. In a back office, one block from Ernest Hemingway's former home in Key West, Florida, and a walk past mirrored walls on a floor paved with salvaged steel complete with a working manhole, is Scott Gilbert's wall of Rubbermaid boxes. They contain Scott's Sweaters, meticulously organized and catalogued. He's an accountant by day, but Scott's been in the sweater business for decades. Scott's Sweaters isn't open to the public, not physically. But he keeps constant vigil maintaining his two websites of men's and women's vintage sweaters at scottssweaters.com and inspirational sweater images at sweaterbaron.com.

Scott's trove of hirsute sweaters consists mostly of vintage mohair and angora ranging in style from après ski to full-blown Muppet. In 2000, eBay propelled his business forward, leading him to create his own online store. For that he needed photography, and he began taking pictures of locals as models.

The terms "lifestyle" and "subculture" are insufficient to describe the enigmatic fashion aesthetic Scott's photos depict. Shades of Paulina Olowska and Bruce Weber are found in the knit of a flocculent white bodysuit against a black velvet backdrop and worn by a provincial but graceful lad of say . . . twenty? The combination of blurry mohair knitted from the fleece of Angora goats, a splash of acne on a young model, and the visible camaraderie of an intergenerational queer community modeling the warmest natural fibers known to man—in the subtropics—is Scott's photographic *je ne sais quoi*.

Scott is a self-taught photographer, but a review of his extensive online oeuvre of sweater photographs helps one to understand how he honed his gaze. The Sweater Baron website contains hundreds of photographs including men's knitwear patterns from the 20th century, stills from "the best sweater movies ever," found images from the web, and Scott's own dot-com advertorial pictures. Deep in the archive are a few backlit portraits of Ricky Schroder showing off both his angelic silky hair and the fuzzy shoulder horizon of the young actor's mohair sweater. Scott has mastered this brushed and backlit technique and refers to it as capturing the "aura" of a sweater.

It's only after researching other high sweater sites such as Milena Bunalova's designs for Dukyana that I begin to see where the utopian principles of Internet communities mesh with the provocative sumptuousness of fetish. The art of Scott's Sweaters is not its off-key context, but in the way the sweaters can wink with a million furry lashes. Scott's Sweaters is a cruise across an illuminated juncture of both physical and photographic fuzziness, seen through eyes watery from vintage pullover, computer screens, and sun drench.

boyer   **travis**

marc camille chaimowicz: design for living

Design is control—typically benevolent, occasionally utopian. But design, by its most base definition, is also force: to assign in thought or intention; to intend for a definite purpose; to plan form and structure.

Marc Camille Chaimowicz constructs environments. He makes furniture. He forms sculptures. He plans performances and installations. There are drawings, collage, photography, ceramics, rugs, folding screens, writing, and videos. Stylistically there is an interest in soft and languid pastels (lilac, mint green, peach), in pattern, decor, texture, and textiles. There is a strong French influence, especially a literary one: Genet, Proust, Cocteau.

His prints seem to be rooted in the painterly vocabulary of the French as well, in that of modernism, and in the curves and crisp graphics of the Wiener Werkstätte and Jugendstil patterns, though emptied of historical authenticity and resurrected through the sherbet palette of mid-century Los Angeles or Miami Deco. They are used for wallpaper, carpets, and textiles. They may also cover entire walls or feature heavily as components in the artist's publications.

It is worth noting Chaimowicz's observation here, taken from his preface to the artist's publication *The World of Interiors* (2007), named and fashioned after the selfsame shelter magazine:

> In common with more pedestrian generic magazines, the domestic spaces featured in *The World of Interiors* are invariably free of occupants.... This not merely affords the stylist greater scope to rearrange, to distance the day-to-day and thus to accentuate various possible fictions—it more importantly enables the readers the better to project themselves into a range of aspirational fantasies....
>
> The exception is that of artists' homes which invariably feature the artist. It is as though these are seen either as extensions of their work or might in some fashion elucidate insight....

In what he refers to as "choreographies," Chaimowicz's work is continuously defined by a controlled ambiguity; what we are allowed (and conversely, disallowed) to view and experience, as well as a refusal to participate in the distinction between presence and absence, representation and abstraction, form and function, craft and art, public and domestic space, and a seemingly ambivalent attitude toward an understanding of the relationship between public and private culture. Throughout his career, his work has often walked an indistinct line between consumer item and art object.

We may be invited inside, but certain rooms remain either just out of sight, or closed off to us altogether.

Marc Camille Chaimowicz. *Working Drawing for a Carpet*, 1992.

konyha　　　　　　　　　　　　　　　　　　　　　　　　**keehnan**

franco albini's "a room for a man"

But the two rooms differ in their choice of materials. Lihotzky favored traditional woods for hers, while Albini constructed his from the latest forms of tubular steel, foam rubber, linoleum, and glass. The result, which looks alluringly sleek, light, and disciplined to a contemporary eye, must have appeared startlingly so in the mid-1930s. Yet Albini also added nuance in the subtle contrast between his industrial materials and the references to traditional Italian architecture in the opulent marble on the walls and floor.

The same qualities would characterize Albini's work until his death in 1977. His most famous furniture designs, like the Veliero and LB7 shelving systems, share a similar delicacy and clarity, yet were combined in his own homes with old masters' paintings and exquisitely crafted antiques. Albini remained dedicated to research, once devoting fifteen years to developing different versions of an armchair and eventually extending his experiments with technocratic materials into rustic ones, like rattan.

So committed was Albini that he continued his investigations throughout World War II, when he left Milan for the smaller city of Piacenza. Bereft of commercial commissions, he sealed himself off in a small studio to reinvent the type of multifunctional furniture he had unveiled to such acclaim in "A Room for a Man," this time using scraps of metal, wood, and whatever else he could find in war-torn Italy.

rawsthorn   alice

There have been some wonderful moments at successive Milan Triennales, the bumper exhibitions of modern design, architecture, and decorative art held (roughly) every three years for much of the 20th century. Among the ones I'd love to have seen were the spectacle of a gleaming Citroën DS 19 dangling from the ceiling of the 1957 exhibition, the student protests that disrupted the 1968 event, and one of the most imposing exhibits, "A Room for a Man" devised by the Italian designer Franco Albini for the 1936 Triennale.

Barely in his thirties, Albini was then at the start of his career, having opened a design studio in Milan a few years before, after working for one of his university teachers, the Italian architect Gio Ponti. So generous was Ponti that he helped Albini establish his practice by championing his early projects in *Domus*, the design and architecture magazine he edited. His support seems even more selfless given that his influence on Albini was waning as the younger designer became enthralled by the rationalist principles of modernism.

Albini's approach to rationalism was engagingly idiosyncratic. What made his work so special was his ability to create objects and spaces that infused the modernist virtues of clarity, economy, and efficiency with elegance, subtlety, and adroit historical references: "A Room for a Man" a prime example.

Like fellow modernists, Albini was committed to exploiting technological innovation to enable people to enjoy the speed and convenience of modern life. Saving time was a key concern, especially when it involved eliminating domestic drudgery, and the possibility of living in a compact space where all essential facilities were easily accessible would have seemed highly desirable.

Somehow, Albini succeeded in squeezing everything he considered necessary for a man living alone into little more than three hundred square feet. Progressive though he was in other respects, he does not seem to have considered that his fictitious client might wish to cook, but did provide places where "he" could work, relax, sleep, and shower.

There is a precedent for Albini's design in the bedsitting room devised in Vienna a decade before by the Austrian architect Margarete Schütte-Lihotzky for a single woman. Both projects make the most of very little space, notably by ensuring that each element fulfills several functions. In Albini's room, the ladder leading up to the bed doubles as a clothes rack and the bed itself as a screen, while a bookshelf turns into a table.

grete lihotzky's bedsitter

No wonder that when the German architect Ernst May saw Lihotzky's work in Vienna, he invited her to join a team of architects charged with constructing more than ten thousand homes in Frankfurt over the following five years. After designing her famous kitchen there, she worked on schools and student housing projects, and married one of her colleagues, Wilhelm Schütte.

But in 1930, with the Nazis gaining power, the Schütte-Lihotzkys fled Germany to join May in the Soviet Union, where he was designing new cities. They remained there until 1937, when they sought refuge in London, Paris, and, finally, Istanbul. When World War II began, Lihotzky joined the Austrian Communist resistance movement only to be arrested and imprisoned in Germany. After being freed by U.S. troops in 1945, she lived in Bulgaria before returning to Austria in 1947.

As a Communist, she was excluded from major architectural commissions, and it was not until the late 1970s that the Austrian authorities finally acknowledged her contribution to the wartime resistance. Then in her eighties, Lihotzky was too old to resume her architectural career, but could, at least, enjoy the reappraisal of her youthful achievements before her death at 102 in 2000. By then, the Frankfurt Kitchen was exhibited at the MAK – Austrian Museum of Applied Arts / Contemporary Art in Vienna, where her beautifully restored bedsitter is now displayed too.

rawsthorn alice

No history of 20th-century design would be complete without a glowing reference to the Frankfurt Kitchen, the model modern kitchen whose late 1920s design was inspired by ship galleys and railway dining cars, as well as by meticulous time-and-motion studies of the dreariest domestic chores.

Compelling though the Frankfurt Kitchen still seems, not least as most contemporary kitchens owe something to it, my favorite work by its designer, the Austrian architect Margarete Schütte-Lihotzky (or Grete Lihotzky, as she preferred to be called), is a humbler project with many of the same qualities. It is the bedsitting room she designed in 1925 in Vienna as a place where a modern woman like herself could read, work, relax, and chat to friends.

Unusual as it was for a woman to have such a room at the time, it would have been deemed even odder of her to ask another woman to design it, and not only because there were so few female architects to choose from.

Grete Lihotzky was among them, and even she would have been unable to pursue an architectural career without her family's connections. Born in Vienna in 1897, she became one of the first women to study architecture at what is now known as the University of Applied Arts Vienna, but only after her mother coaxed a mutual friend into persuading the artist Gustav Klimt to endorse her application.

As a student, Lihotzky won several prizes and was taken under the wing of her professor Oskar Strnad. Other would-be female architects of her generation, like Eileen Gray and Charlotte Perriand, had to start out in the conventionally "feminine" field of interior design, but as soon as Lihotzky graduated Strnad hired her to work on building projects. She was equally fortunate in beginning her career during the "Red Vienna" era, when the city was governed by progressive politicians who championed social and economic experiments, including radical approaches to architecture.

Lihotzky flung herself into developing new forms of housing, including the bedsitting room, which was designed for Karoline Neubacher, wife of the Viennese politician Hermann Neubacher, and installed in their home on Ruhrhofergasse. Its design combines the modernist values of economy, resilience, and simplicity with the formal elegance of pale blue upholstery and opulent walnut veneer. Most of the furniture fulfills several functions, like the bed that doubles as a sofa and storage unit, and a wall panel that drops down to form a desk. Chic, compact, and ingenious, her design is a perfect example of the "Room of One's Own" that the novelist Virginia Woolf claimed was essential for a woman writer in her eponymous 1929 essay.

d for decorator

A mere *decorator* is not how most designers necessarily want to perceive themselves. Yet what's the big deal? Is anything fundamentally wrong with being a decorator? Architect Adolf Loos proclaimed ornament is sin in his essay "Ornament and Crime," an attack on late 19th-century Art Nouveau, but in truth decoration and ornamentation are no more sinful than purity is supremely virtuous.

Take, for example, the psychedelic style of the late 1960s that was smothered in flamboyant ornamentation (indeed much of it borrowed from Loos's dread Art Nouveau). It was nonetheless a revolutionary graphic language used as a code for a revolutionary generation, which is the same role Art Nouveau played seventy years earlier with its vituperative rejection of antiquated 19th-century academic verities.

Decoration is not inherently good or bad. While frequently applied to conceal faulty merchandise and flawed concepts, it nonetheless can improve a product when used with integrity. A decorator does not simply move elements around to achieve an intangible or intuitive goal, but rather optimizes materials at hand to tap into an aesthetic allure and instill a certain kind of pleasure.

Often playing an integral role in the total design scheme, decoration is not merely wallpaper. Good decoration is that which frames a product or message. One should never underestimate the power of decoration to stimulate. It takes as much sophistication to be a decorator as it does a conceptualizer. The worst decorative excesses are not the obsessively baroque borders and patterns that are born of an eclectic vision but the ignorant application of dysfunctional anachronistic doodads. A splendidly ornamented package may cost a little more to produce but have quantifiable impact on the consumers with discerning tastes who buy them (and sometimes keep the boxes after the product is used up).

No decoration is truly sinful, though sometimes it is trivial. Yet to practice the decorative arts does not a priori relegate one to inferior status, branded with a scarlet and floriated letter *D*. Some designers are great because they are exemplary decorators.

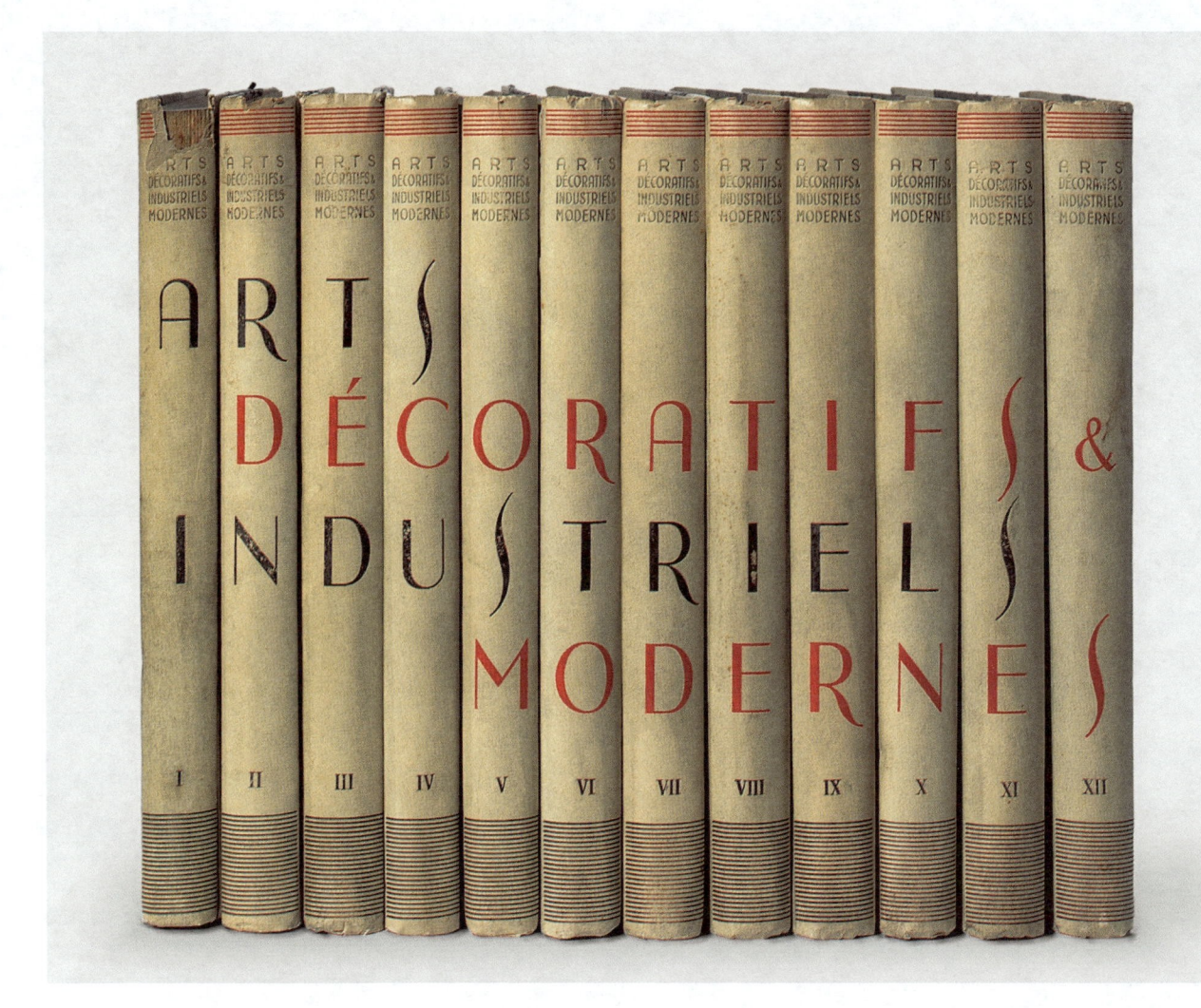

heller **steven**

"in a remote place not far from here i was looking for shelter."

These are the first words in the book called *Shelter*. From 2006 to 2011, Dutch photographer Henk Wildschut traveled back and forth between Amsterdam and Calais, the departure point for emigrants hoping to cross illegally into the U.K., moving as well from his own safe haven into the vulnerable situation of the waiting emigrants holed up in tents. In doing so, he found a way to convey the harsh beauty he found in these settings; in discreetly photographing from a distance, he has made the scenery even more striking.

These "still lifes" are closely observed without his touching a hair, in contrast to our own photographic still lifes, which are painstakingly constructed inch by inch, from the camera's point of view. These are different routes yet they have a common ground in which form has followed function.

The drapes of fabric emphasized by snow propose both a painterly canvas and a stark document of the cold and misery endured by the emigrants. Its dramatic beauty is not sentimental. In photographing these temporary hidden spots, Henk Wildschut has made them into a memorial about despair and the power to survive at the border of Calais, where shelters come and go.

Henk Wildschut. *Shelter, Calais, France, February 2009.*

scheltens and abbenes

maurice and liesbeth

making and manufacturing

A few years ago I had the opportunity to publish books with two designers whom I have admired for some time: Ted Muehling and Greg Lynn. On the surface, their work could not be more different. Ted's works are revered for their delicate, nature-inspired sensibilities: impossibly fragile hand-painted blown crystal for Lobmeyr, handworked, intricate porcelain pieces for Nymphenburg, and of course the seemingly simple yet highly coveted silver and gold earrings and necklaces that adorn every stylish woman in New York and Paris. Greg, by contrast, was one of the enfants terribles of the digital movement once known as "blob architecture." By employing advanced digital technologies borrowed from the aerodynamic industries, Greg generates forms that are by definition "futuristic." While waiting for the building industry to play catch-up, Greg's non-theoretical output has included imagery and designs for Hollywood sci-fi films.

By sheer chance, at the end of the collaborations both Ted and Greg gifted me, as a memento, a spoon of their design. (Perhaps it wasn't truly coincidence, as both knew that I am rather obsessed with flatware—both their forms and their manufacturing processes.) For me these two artifacts perfectly capture the philosophy of each designer's body of work. The handcrafted spoon by Ted has a silver bowl attached to a blackened bronze handle, cast from a bayberry branch Ted collected from his yard in Sag Harbor; by nature and by design, each spoon is unique, literally one of a kind. Greg's spoon, on the other hand, is made using the cutting-edge manufacturing method of rapid prototyping: after the piece is finalized in a three-dimensional design software, the product is stereolithographically printed by lasers from a bath of sintered steel and bronze particles. Other than the printer, no other tools were employed.

It would be simple—and simplistic—to set these two methodologies in opposition (and, depending on your disposition, choose the romance of the pre-industrial craft over the seduction of the hi-tech ethos). For me, both exist as truly viable and coeval modes of production (they do sit side by side in my living room, as a daily reminder and proof of this coexistence).

The postwar Italian architects, faced with the unprecedented task of rebuilding their devastated cities, developed a new manifesto of the design professional, someone who can address our needs at all scales, "from the spoon to the city." The future of *our* built environment will need to partake of the two methodologies embodied here, and it starts with spoons.

ngo   **dung**

the mies van der rohe archive

I never met Mies van der Rohe, but no other single individual has had a greater impact on my architectural thinking, with the exception perhaps of the Japanese designer Shiro Kuramata. I remember visiting the Robert F. Carr Memorial Chapel of Saint Savior at the Illinois Institute of Technology some years ago and noticing how the floor grid precisely bisects a stainless steel rail. Mies can get away with this sort of exactness that elsewhere tends to produce a sort of tension, because his work is perfect.

The Mies van der Rohe Archive is an illustrated catalog of the architect's drawings held by the Museum of Modern Art, published in twenty volumes between 1986 and 1992, the first six covering the German projects and the remaining fourteen devoted to the American work. This vast editorial undertaking was begun by the great Arthur Drexler, curator and director of the department of art and design at MoMA, and completed after Drexler's death by writer and architecture critic Franz Schulze. The collected material for a single house can fill an entire volume, offering unparalleled insights into the way Mies subjected his early ideas to a rigorous process of examination and reexamination, as he sought to satisfy his own requirements for absolute refinement. The briefest handwritten annotation and the broadest of pencil strokes on tracing paper can convey so much.

There is something very reassuring about the physical presence of these books in my office and I find myself regularly taking down a volume—whether in search of something in particular, or simply for the pleasure of browsing.

Illinois Institute of Technology Chapel of St. Savior.

pawson john

french curves

I've always called them "French curves." But they are probably more correctly referred to as "ship's curves," as they were most often used to achieve the lines needed to build boats. Although I don't remember how I came to have them, they may have belonged to my grandfather. When I began working as a designer I used them to draw non-radial curves, like a door handle I designed for FSB in 1989. The arrow marks and zeros visible on some of them were made by me while drawing segments of longer curves. Nowadays computer drawing programs are equipped with everything you need to achieve a smooth and precise curve, but the process feels detached and inhuman compared to the physical sensation of running your pen along a well-curved plane of wood. It's no exaggeration to say that these shapes helped develop my sense of line and appreciation of form itself. Someone else made them, but in doing so they passed on something far more important than a tool for drawing curves.

morrison

jasper

cherub

He had been standing on the roof longer than he could remember. The sun had turned his skin burning hot, the wind had thrummed against him, and the rain had sounded across his body like drums. At first it had been exciting—the call for auditions, when he'd proudly displayed his plump outline and practiced classical stance; and then being chosen as one of only a very few to stand above the crowds, to be admired and photographed for all eternity . . . or as long as his body held out. Ay, there's the rub. His once smooth, bronzed body: first it developed this sickly patina, then the spots that grew to giant welts. He'd noticed it on the others first—with sidelong glances he marked the change in them—but due to his pose there wasn't much he could see of himself. But yes, he could see his chest growing green. He felt the welts and by looking at the others guessed what they were. It was ironic that he'd been chosen for his purity and beauty only to become a symbol of death and decay. People who had once wondered at his form now exclaimed in pity. Pity! His wings ached and the place where they joined his body felt thin and weak. One day they would fall right off and he would be taken down—cast down from the heavens to hell: to some smelting fire, no doubt to be reformed . . . into a garden ornament, he hoped. It would be a goddamned relief.

bantjes   **marian**

floors i like

Few museums in the world have endured such radical ideological transformations as the Haus der Kunst in Munich. Commissioned by Adolf Hitler in 1933, it was the first in a series of buildings intended to promote National Socialist ideals. Baptized "Haus der Deutschen Kunst" (House of German Art), it served as a propaganda tool to showcase "pure" Aryan art. At the end of World War II, it was seized by U.S. troops, who removed most of the Nazi symbols, dropped the "German" from its name, and transformed it into a social club for military personnel, complete with an interior basketball court. Before becoming Munich's modern-art museum, it underwent several metamorphoses—including a stint as a trade-show venue—amid recurrent public calls for its demolition. Indeed, it was not until a significant renovation in the early 1990s and the arrival of non-German directors such as Christoph Vitali and Chris Dercon that the Haus der Kunst finally evolved from an unwelcome reminder of a dreadful past into a forward-thinking hub for modern and contemporary art.

The Haus der Kunst's architect was Paul Ludwig Troost, at the time the Führer's favorite. Inside the forbidding, rigidly symmetrical exterior, Troost used copious amounts of Tegernsee marble—a bloodred, heavily veined limestone—to cover walls and floors to dramatic effect (as shown here) in the northeastern staircase. Since the building's completion in 1937, everyone from Adolf Hitler and Joseph Goebbels to Paul McCarthy and Gilbert & George has left his or her figurative footprints on this symbolically charged surface. With the directorship of acclaimed Nigerian-born curator Okwui Enwezor, the Haus der Kunst began yet another exciting metamorphosis. And those bloodred limestone floors were still there to witness it.

burrichter   **felix**

vlisco

La Famille is an archetypal Vlisco design—persistently popular since its inception in 1952—with dazzling colors, an eye-catching rhythmic pattern, and a luxurious feel. The textile represents the traditional family: mother (hen), father (rooster head), children (chicks), and future children (eggs). The irony of this "happy family" is depicted in the repeated motif of the rooster head—the absent body of the father being a metaphor for the husband's failure to satisfy his wife, and she is, in return, unfaithful to him.

Many Vlisco graphics narrate moral tales or depict ceremonial customs while others reference contemporary pop-culture motifs such as USB cords and common objects like high heels and envelopes. There are even commemorative cloths featuring portraits of presidents and British royalty. Some prints are purely ornamental, leaning toward the botanical, geometric, and abstract, but all are consistently vibrant with electric shapes and piercing color combinations.

The story of Vlisco and the origin of the *véritable wax hollandais* (French for "real Dutch wax") are rooted in a diverse chain of cultural influences and colonial meetings. Vlisco was founded in Haarlem, the Netherlands, in 1846 by Dutch merchant Pieter Fentener van Vlissingen. He first encountered batik textiles in the Dutch colony of Indonesia and saw great potential in their unique printed quality. Batik is a form of wax-resist printing in which hot wax is applied to areas of a cloth before dyeing to resist color. Through the process of repeated dyeing, the wax begins to crack, resulting in a layered *craquelé* effect. Vlissingen brought this technique to the Netherlands and produced batik fabrics that were sold back to the Indonesian market. Vlisco copied and adapted indigenous colors and motifs, which were strongly related to status and occasion, in response to market preferences.

After sales decreased in Indonesia, Vlisco moved its business to West Africa in the late 19th century. After all, Dutch merchants had been trading fabrics in West Africa successfully for two hundred years. However, competition from other distributors forced Vlisco to change its direction: colors became brighter and regional patterns were incorporated into the designs. Local merchants sold Vlisco prints to well-off African women, who then sewed the material into garments. The company prospered in West Africa and, by the 1950s, the fabrics were so deeply integrated into African society that they became a symbol of African identity—despite the inherent paradox.

Today, cheaper knock-offs have flooded the African market and Vlisco has had to develop new strategies to maintain its position as the leading textile distributor. Vlisco continues to offer a collection of designs that have proved their popularity over time—attending to their loyal customers—while new prints, made with collaborating artists, are introduced every three months. Nonetheless, the Vlisco customer can distinguish the original from its cheap counterfeit, and thus the *véritable wax hollandais* remains close to the hearts of many African women who have adorned themselves in Vlisco for generations. Although this particular Dutch-African hybrid emerged from a cultural crossbreeding, it remains central to African identity and pride. The woman who now wears Vlisco is modern and cosmopolitan and has, of course, great fashion sense.

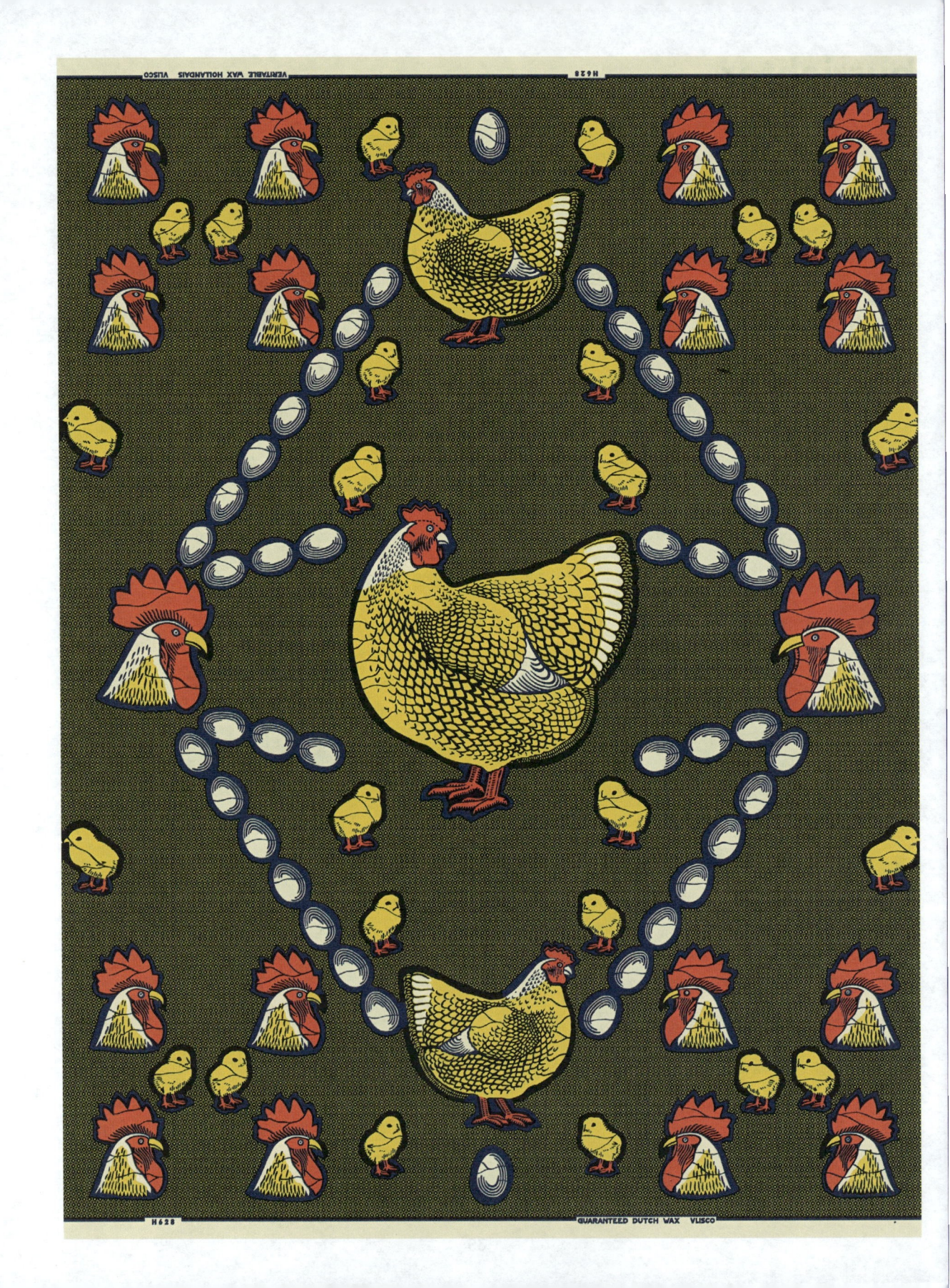

Ted van de Ven. La Famille, 1952.

liemburg   **harmen**

the liar

Like a successful joke, it takes two to birth a successful lie—the liar and the lied-to. Each player must be well cast; each participant has a role to play. If you are going to tell a good lie, it is important that the lie, however outrageous, be hauntingly *plausible*. Even if the lie is planted at the very edge of credulity, and all it takes is the gentlest wind of clearheadedness to catapult the liar into the unrecoverable shame of disbelief, a good lie will deactivate the psychological and emotional defense system of the lied-to so that the lie withstands scrutiny, and, regardless, cannot be uprooted. An elegant lie is also a challenge—a black-tie dare, a glove in the face—made by the liar to the lied-to: *"Are you absolutely certain I'm lying?"* A good lie doesn't require the "benefit of the doubt"; a good lie relies on the cowardice of the lied-to to put *all* of their chips on the story. Good lying is an art; great lying is a gift. Mr. N. had the gift. For five years, Mr. N. was our floor waxer at our loft residence as well as the first little Moss store. He was a brilliant floor waxer: like a butler polishing the silver, Mr. N. polished our floors, with butcher's wax applied on hands and knees. We used to slide and fall constantly, he was that good. But as good a waxer as he was, Mr. N. was an even better liar. And I was an excellent lied-to partner. And every month, for years, we had hours to play out the roles we were born into. It first began with "I've started a lemonade franchise, and it's going national." "How about that," I said to my partner, Franklin. "Isn't that just wonderful . . . inspiring?!" It didn't ring true, but my entire value system was based on the plausibility of "anyone can become president." I was the benefactor, big time, of my grandparents' trust in America's gold-lined streets. I had cousins whom I'd never met, living (I was told) impoverished in Romania. I was, let's just say, in quite different circumstances. In my world, Cinderella was a real person. So you can understand, I hope, how invested I was in the plausibility of Mr. N.'s lemonade franchise. A year or so passed, then came: "I've been hired by American *Vogue* as a columnist." This played out over two years. "When's your first story being published?" I said. "Blah blah blah . . ." Mr. N. would reply, time and again. Franklin kept silent. Many dressy lies followed: dinners with Anna . . . a TV series under discussion. . . . You get my drift. Finally, in our fifth year: "I was very good friends with Jackie Onassis. Did you know she wore a men's size 12 shoe?" I remember sharing this with Franklin, and the earth-shattering, coldhearted, there-is-no-Santa-Claus SCREAM in reply: "He's a LIAR. Murray, do you hear me? He's a LIAR." Our lives are touched in many different ways. There are many different ways we each might respond. Franklin and I installed wall-to-wall. The "impossible" became plausible.

Maurizio Cattelan. *Daddy Daddy*, 2008.

moss   **murray**

willem sandberg's
experimenta typografica

Sandberg produced nineteen pamphlets between December 1943 and April 1945, making a couple of copies of each one, all done by hand. They consisted of twenty to sixty pages of drawings, collages, and texts, which were either written by Sandberg himself or quoted from Confucius, Proudhon, Stendhal, and other favorite writers on themes like love, death, education, architecture, and typography. As Sandberg had no money and materials were scarce in wartime, he improvised by using whatever he could find: scraps of wallpaper, cardboard packaging, tissue paper, and wrapping paper together with photographs, drawings, and symbols torn from magazines for his collages.

The pamphlets were to be printed in Amsterdam by Sandberg's friend and co-conspirator, Frans Duwaer, but he was arrested and killed by the Gestapo. Instead the *Experimenta Typographica* were printed first by the Vijpondpers, or "5lb Press"—so called because the Nazis banned the production of publications using more than five pounds of paper—and, later, by an art gallery in Cologne.

Just as Sandberg's reflections as a fugitive had a profound influence on his directorship of the Stedelijk, his ingenious use of found materials, esoteric typefaces, vivid colors, and lowercase lettering in the *Experimenta Typographica* defined the visual identity of the museum as well as reminds us of his courage and resourcefulness.

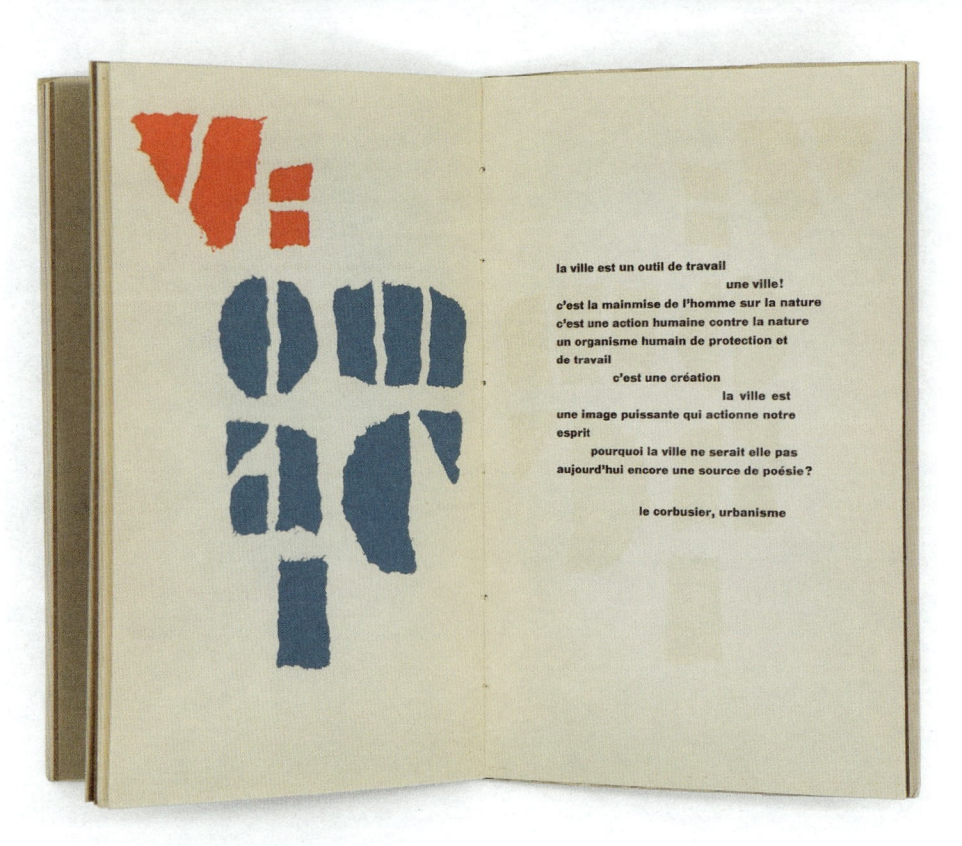

rawsthorn   alice

One glance at the exhibition posters from the late 1940s and 1950s lining a wall of the Stedelijk Museum in Amsterdam is enough to see how dynamic it was at that time, both in celebrating the history of the avant-garde and championing new artists.

The Stedelijk owes its reputation as one of the most influential modern art museums of the postwar era to Willem Sandberg, its director from 1945 to 1963. If all he had done was discharge his directorial duties, Sandberg would still be revered as a great museologist, but he also fulfilled an unofficial role as the Stedelijk's graphic designer, producing hundreds of posters and catalog during his directorship, as well as the museum's stationery and tickets.

Self-taught though Sandberg was in design, he developed a distinctive visual language for the Stedelijk characterized by the clarity and economy of simple forms and bold colors. The roots of his design sensibility, described by his friend and fellow designer Jan Bons as a "cheerful minimum," are also on display there: a series of pamphlets entitled *Experimenta Typografica* that he made in a perilous period when he was on the run from the Nazis, living secretly in the Dutch countryside during World War II.

Born to a wealthy family in the Dutch city of Amersfoort in 1897, Sandberg studied art in Amsterdam before traveling around Europe, living in Paris and Vienna, visiting the Bauhaus art and design school in Germany, and serving a printing apprenticeship in Switzerland. Shortly after returning to Amsterdam, he started working for the Stedelijk as a graphic designer and curator.

When the Nazis occupied the Netherlands in 1940, Sandberg joined the resistance, applying his design and printing skills to forge identity papers and using his professional status at the museum to meet in secret with dissident groups on official visits to Germany. In 1943, he was part of a plot to destroy the official records at the Amsterdam Central Civil Registry Office. He and his co-conspirators were betrayed and forced to go into hiding. All of the others were eventually captured by the Gestapo and sentenced to death.

Having disguised his appearance, Sandberg spent the last fifteen months of the war in the tiny town of Gennep in the eastern Netherlands posing as Henri Willem van der Bosch. With Sandberg living hand to mouth under a false identity and knowing that his wife was in prison, their son was in a concentration camp, and many of his friends were dead, his hair went white. He sought solace in reading, mostly on art and philosophy, recording his observations in the *Experimenta Typografica*.

head of the virgin

Great care and artistry went into the creation of this carved and painted ivory head of the Virgin Mary. It was once part of an exceptionally oversized *santos* figure from the early 20th-century Philippines. Being larger than most *santos* —standing about four feet in height—this statuary is also more lavishly decorated. Her ivory skin has been tinted with a rose-colored flush, her lips painted pink, and long lashes made from boar's hair have been applied to the lids of her shadowed glass eyes. Although her hairline is painted, she would have worn a wig of long tresses fashioned from human hair or corn silk.

A figure of this size, requiring a substantially large ivory tusk, must have been very costly to make. The repair on her neck, which was likely at one point hidden by a high-necked dress collar, possibly indicates an irregularity in the ivory remedied by a patch carved from another piece. The Virgin's ears are pierced, and her earrings, in likeness to the originals, were designed using gold beads from an antique Philippine *tamborin* necklace. The Virgin is also adorned with a 19th-century engraved silver crown—originally made for a similar *santos* figure— which is embellished with brilliant rose-cut diamonds, creating a sparkling corona.

de vera   **federico**

weeds in the drawing room

Sometimes avant-garde acts of a past era become so subsumed into contemporary culture, so ubiquitously emulated, that in retrospect their genius is overlooked. Such is the case with Constance Spry, the reformer of flower decoration (Spry's own term to set her work apart from traditional floristry), which became the province of middle-class women. Spry was the modernist of her métier. Her gentle yet radically unorthodox assemblages are not generally recognized as such today, though the beauty of her ephemeral art inspires contemporary aesthetics. Spry can best be remembered as doing the flowers for London society from the 1930s to the 1950s, just as Cecil Beaton snapped society portraits and Syrie Maugham whitewashed society drawing rooms; this tripartite glamour ruled during the periods that bracketed World War II. Spry was also a social equalizer and a parvenu; her employees in pink overalls used the front door, not the tradesman's entrance, when they came to install at clients' homes. She was a proto-feminist entrepreneur who brought real mettle to a feminine pastime and a bohemian whose liaison with the cross-dressing lesbian painter Gluck (whose best work is of Spry's still lifes) lent to all her work a tang of sensuality.

Spry raged against the Victorian hangover of carnations garnished with fern in cut-glass vases to be dotted around the room, and instead presented architectural showpieces spilling forth from alabaster urns, her own papier-mâché creations, or whitewashed junk shop finds (harmonizing with Syrie). Their contents: a wild mix of meadow weeds and stuff from the vegetable patch hitherto unthinkable alongside white lilies, orchids, and other exotics. Famously, sensationally, for a Mayfair perfumer's window she paired scarlet roses with red kale to such an effect that the police had to be called for crowd control. Spry democratized flowers, branches, and all vegetation in service to decorative beauty, though at the same time she was an artificer, wire-rigging stems and divesting leaves to banish any unintended results. She orchestrated the spectacle of flowers for Queen Elizabeth's coronation (which could have perhaps been done by another), but Spry was also the woman who, in a sublime gesture to lift morale during the Blitz, instructed the public on how to make an arrangement from the flowers that sprung from the scorched earth of London's fresh bombsites—a conceptualist act and an homage to the magenta of fireweed.

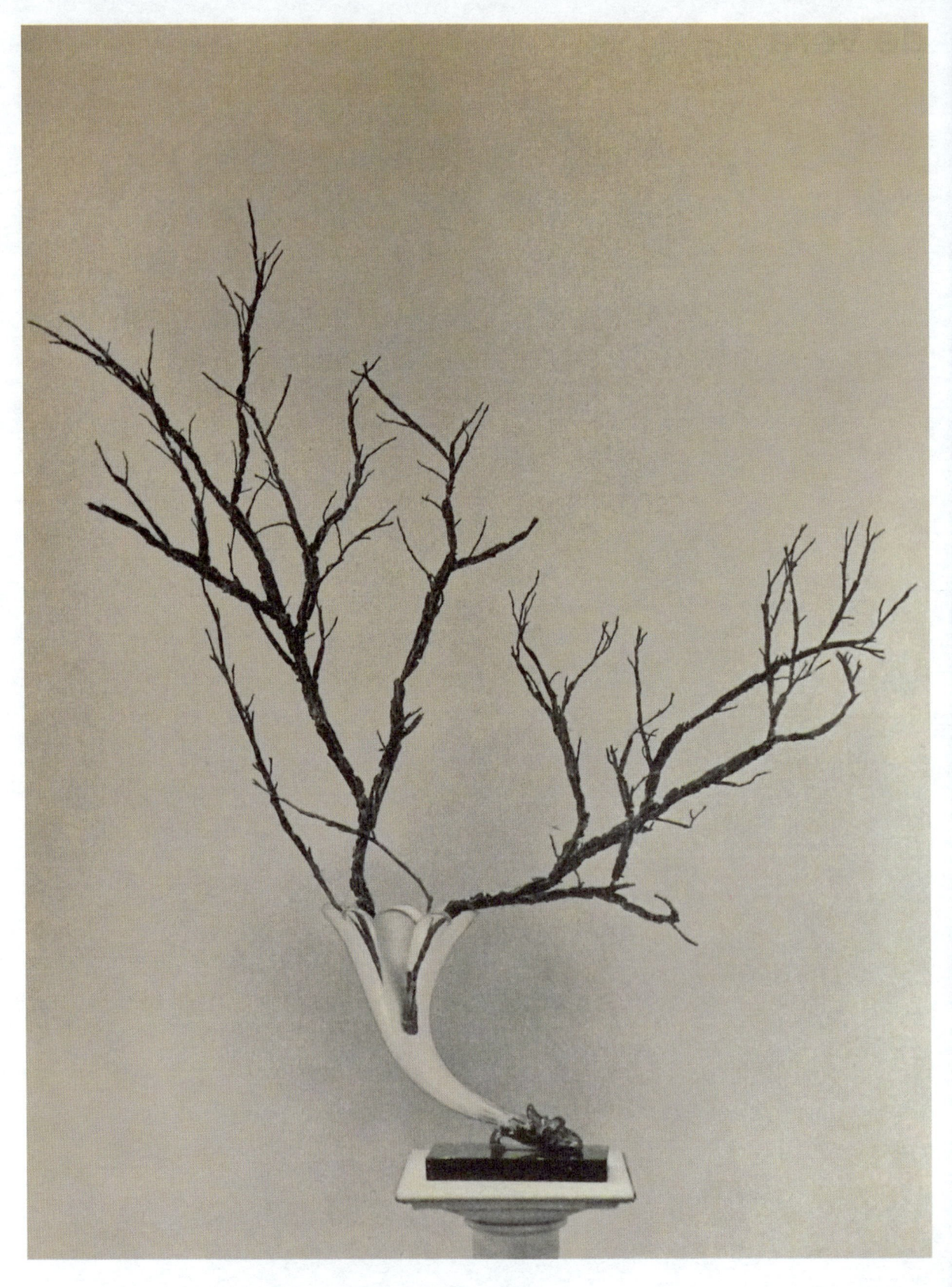

p. **paul**

four stories

I am always wanting to deaccession,
but packets keep arriving that bring great joy.
Here are three gifts and a chicken.

cloth watch

The watch was made in Laos. You tie it to your wrist. When you wear it, you have all the time in the world. There is a great comfort in that, of course.

chicken

I lived in Rome for three months and went to Florence only once. To eat lunch in a restaurant famous for this boiled chicken. So I went to Florence to eat this chicken. And I have to tell you, the chicken sat on the plate, sparse and spare as a short story.

kalman

maira

funnel

This funnel costs $1.95. It could have been porcelain, but it is plastic. It sits on the table next to the metal funnel from India and another white funnel from Colorado. Like Band-Aids, you can never have enough funnels.

absolutely no visitors

The sign could have read NO VISITORS. But someone thought that it needed the ABSOLUTELY. Absolutely right.

night and day

I departed, quite upset over the outcome since I had offered to make a strike off but he wouldn't wait for one, and told him to "never darken our door again" (actually, it was something a bit stronger as to what he could do with his next bunny fur order). I then proceeded to make another two trips down the four flights of stairs.

I decided not to confess anything to my superiors until I could find a buyer and, fortuitously, I found a belt manufacturer from whom I was thrilled to get $1.05/yard for all one thousand yards, which left me feeling that life was once again worth living.

Approximately two years passed then my phone rang and a familiar voice said, "Don? Jack. Do you have fake mink?" My immediate retort was, "Fake mink? F___ you!" and I hung up the phone.

In the rose-colored retrospect of sixty years, I owe a debt of gratitude to Jack Kukoff and the frightening prospect of a lifetime of leopard-printed bunny fur for inspiring the beginnings of the Maharam you know today.

Donald Maharam pictured with client, ca. 1960.

maharam

donald

To put time and money into perspective, I graduated from college in 1952 and my starting salary in the family business, lorded over by my father and his three brothers, was $50.00/week, netting a very impressive $37.12 after taxes.

With nothing in the form of organized guidance, I was told to "start learning the business and all the departments." At that time, we sold costume and scenic fabrics for the theater trade, along with all the display paraphernalia required for seasonal window displays in retail stores. In addition to some rather mundane office duties, I was the assigned recipient of incoming calls from our smaller accounts, thus my inheritance of Jack Kukoff.

Jack manufactured skirt and sweater sets in a fourth-floor loft space on 14th Street, with a thirty-person sewing pool. Every few months he would call and order a bolt of our "bunny fur," a brushed synthetic fabric that simulated white rabbit. He would die-cut the fabric into bunny shapes—one for the skirt and one for the sweater. Not exactly Chanel, but he had his niche.

In 1953, faux leopard became extremely popular in the fashion industry. Hanora fake fur dominated the market, and demand outstripped supply. I received an "emergency call" from Jack, who wanted to know if we had "fake leopard" in our collection of costume fabrics. I explained that we offered a leopard print on white satin and that we could print this leopard pattern on his bunny fur—our best approach to simulate faux leopard. Jack immediately wanted to know cost and lead time for one thousand yards. The thousand yards of bunny fur was immediately available, and our printer on Manhattan's west side felt he would have no problem printing—all told, the job would take two weeks.

I paid a visit to Jack, who looked at the samples of our satin leopard print and bunny fur rather quickly and said, "Here's an order for one thousand yards, just get it going." Based on a cost of ninety-five cents, I had quoted $1.50 a yard, and he was delighted since, as he pointed out, the "Hanora stuff" cost him $2.25 a yard. I called Hanora that afternoon and found that their faux leopard was, in fact, $4.50 a yard.

Three days after I received his order, the calls began to come on a daily basis . . . "So, where are my goods?" On day ten I was able to deliver four fifty-yard bolts in a cab on a ninety-five degree day at the end of July. Unfortunately, when I arrived at 12:15 p.m., the elevator operator was at lunch and his alternate was out sick. It took two trips up four flights of stairs, one bolt over each shoulder, to deliver the four bolts. Jack opened the first roll and by the look on his face I sensed a problem. He disappeared for a moment and came back with his "$2.25 a yard" Hanora faux leopard. When compared to my printed bunny fur, it was like a Rolls-Royce sitting alongside a Chevrolet. I was hopeful that the price coupled with the urgency of his need would prevail. His only comment was, "Night and day." I countered with, "A wonderful tune by Cole Porter," to which he repeated, "Night and day." I felt obliged to repeat once again, "A wonderful tune by Cole Porter." To my dismay, his third counter was, simply, "I can't use it." It was the ultimate death knell.

maharam stories greet every visitor to our website . . . our effort to supplant the predictable celebration of one's wares with an opportunity to explore.

My father taught us that there were few more important aspirations in life than being interesting and that we would be measured by the substance of our curiosity. Throughout his life, boundless stacks of magazines have been his internet, voyage his muse, and the next, new, odd, and obscure points on his compass. He toiled in his youth to exercise his pride of accomplishment and to provide the platform for the creative expression we enjoy today.

maharam stories was borne of an appreciation for these values.

michael maharam

**to my storyteller,
donald maharam**

maharam

maharam stories
edited by michael maharam with bailey salisbury

Skira *Rizzoli* NEW YORK